THE UNFOLDING CRISIS IN BURUNDI

HEARING

BEFORE THE

SUBCOMMITTEE ON AFRICA, GLOBAL HEALTH, GLOBAL HUMAN RIGHTS, AND INTERNATIONAL ORGANIZATIONS

OF THE

COMMITTEE ON FOREIGN AFFAIRS HOUSE OF REPRESENTATIVES

ONE HUNDRED FOURTEENTH CONGRESS

FIRST SESSION

JULY 22, 2015

Serial No. 114–90

Printed for the use of the Committee on Foreign Affairs

Available via the World Wide Web: http://www.foreignaffairs.house.gov/ or http://www.gpo.gov/fdsys/

U.S. GOVERNMENT PUBLISHING OFFICE

95–635PDF   WASHINGTON : 2015

For sale by the Superintendent of Documents, U.S. Government Publishing Office
Internet: bookstore.gpo.gov   Phone: toll free (866) 512–1800; DC area (202) 512–1800
Fax: (202) 512–2104   Mail: Stop IDCC, Washington, DC 20402–0001

COMMITTEE ON FOREIGN AFFAIRS

EDWARD R. ROYCE, California, *Chairman*

CHRISTOPHER H. SMITH, New Jersey
ILEANA ROS-LEHTINEN, Florida
DANA ROHRABACHER, California
STEVE CHABOT, Ohio
JOE WILSON, South Carolina
MICHAEL T. McCAUL, Texas
TED POE, Texas
MATT SALMON, Arizona
DARRELL E. ISSA, California
TOM MARINO, Pennsylvania
JEFF DUNCAN, South Carolina
MO BROOKS, Alabama
PAUL COOK, California
RANDY K. WEBER SR., Texas
SCOTT PERRY, Pennsylvania
RON DeSANTIS, Florida
MARK MEADOWS, North Carolina
TED S. YOHO, Florida
CURT CLAWSON, Florida
SCOTT DesJARLAIS, Tennessee
REID J. RIBBLE, Wisconsin
DAVID A. TROTT, Michigan
LEE M. ZELDIN, New York
DANIEL DONOVAN, New York

ELIOT L. ENGEL, New York
BRAD SHERMAN, California
GREGORY W. MEEKS, New York
ALBIO SIRES, New Jersey
GERALD E. CONNOLLY, Virginia
THEODORE E. DEUTCH, Florida
BRIAN HIGGINS, New York
KAREN BASS, California
WILLIAM KEATING, Massachusetts
DAVID CICILLINE, Rhode Island
ALAN GRAYSON, Florida
AMI BERA, California
ALAN S. LOWENTHAL, California
GRACE MENG, New York
LOIS FRANKEL, Florida
TULSI GABBARD, Hawaii
JOAQUIN CASTRO, Texas
ROBIN L. KELLY, Illinois
BRENDAN F. BOYLE, Pennsylvania

AMY PORTER, *Chief of Staff*   THOMAS SHEEHY, *Staff Director*
JASON STEINBAUM, *Democratic Staff Director*

————

SUBCOMMITTEE ON AFRICA, GLOBAL HEALTH, GLOBAL HUMAN RIGHTS, AND INTERNATIONAL ORGANIZATIONS

CHRISTOPHER H. SMITH, New Jersey, *Chairman*

MARK MEADOWS, North Carolina
CURT CLAWSON, Florida
SCOTT DesJARLAIS, Tennessee
DANIEL DONOVAN, New York

KAREN BASS, California
DAVID CICILLINE, Rhode Island
AMI BERA, California

CONTENTS

THE UNFOLDING CRISIS IN BURUNDI

WEDNESDAY, JULY 22, 2015

House of Representatives,
Subcommittee on Africa, Global Health,
Global Human Rights, and International Organizations,
Committee on Foreign Affairs,
Washington, DC.

The subcommittee met, pursuant to notice, at 12 o'clock p.m., in room 2200 Rayburn House Office Building, Hon. Christopher H. Smith (chairman of the subcommittee) presiding.

Mr. SMITH. The hearing will come to order. And we will be joined shortly by our distinguished ranking member, so we should just wait for her to begin opening comments. Thank you all for being here, and I especially want to thank our witnesses for their expertise and for the insights I know they will provide to the subcommittee.

Our hearing today is extremely timely as events are unfolding in real time in Burundi, a small nation that is often overlooked by the international community, including those of us here in the U.S. House and Senate.

Many are familiar with the horrific genocidal violence that gripped Rwanda in the 1990s, as Hutu and Tutsi butchered each other in outgrowths of ethnic hatred. Few knew, however, that Burundi was also going through a protracted Tutsi versus Hutu ethnic struggle that also amounted to genocide in the 1990s.

Few knew that Burundi, without much fanfare and without the largess that the international community showered upon Rwanda, overcame its divisive civil war and, following a peace brokered by Nelson Mandela solemnized in the Arusha Accords of 2000, has sought to heal the wounds of the past and rebuild a nation.

Today, however, this peace is under the threat of unraveling. The sitting President of Burundi Pierre Nkurunziza, in apparent defiance of the term limits set forth in the Arusha Accords and memorialized in the Constitution, is seeking a third term. While the constitutional issue is complex and unsettled, the rising political violence and tension—not to mention the roughly 160,000 people displaced and seeking refuge in neighboring countries—is easy to understand and serves as the canary in the coal mine. There are real problems, and again we need to be ahead of this, not behind, in trying to mitigate a crisis.

There is a window of opportunity for action, where immediate and sustained action can prevent the situation from escalating out of control. As in the case of the Central African Republic, about

(1)

which we held two critical hearings in our subcommittee in the last Congress, timely attention and targeted interventions can stop an incipient conflict from metastasizing. Burundi is now approaching a tipping point, though it has yet to topple over.

There is still time, and we in Congress have a role to play in sounding the alarm and prodding the administration to take action followed by oversight. We also need to avoid the temptation to be penny wise and pound foolish. As several of our witnesses will explain, by spending a small amount to further democracy and governance efforts in fragile states such as Burundi, we can avoid much greater cost down the road, and of course the mitigation of the loss of life. And I mean not simply by the dollar and cents expense, but more importantly, like I said, the blood lost and the lives shattered.

In Burundi, the administration must do more. While often-lonely voices such as that of Samantha Power have called attention to the need for atrocity prevention, too often the administration policy has been one of, if not malign neglect then certainly non-benign neglect.

We saw this, for example, in the foot-dragging that accompanied the appointment of a Special Envoy for the Great Lakes Region of Africa. In January of this year, then Special Envoy Russ Feingold announced that he was stepping down. This subcommittee called on the administration to find a replacement as soon as possible, as the circle of violence was beginning to widen in Burundi.

In May, for example, I stated that a failure to do so signaled a ''disengagement when lives are at stake.'' I was afraid that we would see a repeat of the administration's inaction with respect to the Middle East, where to date it has yet to appoint a Special Envoy to Promote Religious Freedom of Religious Minorities in the Near East and South Central Asia despite Congress having created that position last August, almost 1 year ago.

I look forward to the comments and the testimony of our distinguished witnesses. I yield to Ms. Bass.

Ms. BASS. Thank you, Chairman Smith, for calling this meeting and to giving us an opportunity to discuss the current state of affairs in Burundi amid the election violence and the refugee crisis.

Last year, I had the opportunity to meet with President Nkurunziza and I voiced concerns around the stability in the region and feared the current situation. We had a frank conversation around it, and he told me at that time that he felt that there was, because of how he took office, that there was a reason and a rationale for him to run again. And we expressed our concern that the situation that is occurring right now is what would happen if he pursued that course.

I want to offer my appreciation to today's witnesses for agreeing to participate in the hearing. And I can't help myself, but I have to acknowledge the presence of Steve McDonald, who we haven't seen in a while, and I am really happy to know that you are here today and look forward to your testimony.

I want to close quickly because I know we have a short period of time before we are going to be called to vote, but I do want to say that in your testimony I hope you will also give reference to the surrounding countries, the impact on those countries, and then just the outright fear that this could really expand into a region-wide war. With that I yield.

Mr. SMITH. Thank you very much. Mr. Donovan?

Mr. DONOVAN. Mr. Chairman, I will yield my time too. I will be very interested to hear what the witnesses have, and as Ms. Bass said we have a short period of time. So thank you, sir.

Mr. SMITH. Thank you. I will do abbreviated introductions.

Beginning with Mr. Mike Jobbins who is director of global affairs at Search for Common Ground, a conflict transformation organization that has worked on supporting media, community dialogue, and collective actions for peace and reconciliation in Burundi for more than two decades, he has covered the Great Lakes Region for 10 years, most recently a senior program manager for Africa at Search.

Mr. Jobbins previously lived in Burundi and the DRC and worked on the region as a program associate at the Woodrow Wilson Center. He previously testified before our committee on the Central African Republic.

We will then hear from Dr. Elavie Ndura who is a tenured professor of education and immediate past academic program coordinator of the multilingual/multicultural education program in George Mason University's College of Education and Human Development. She was a 2010–11 fellow at the Woodrow Wilson International Center for Scholars and recipient of the Peace and Justice Association's 2011 Peace Educator of the Year Award. Dr. Ndura was a Fulbright Scholar, and the recipient of the British Council Scholarship. She is the founder and coordinator of the Burundi Schools Project and author of several books on peacekeeping in Africa.

Then we will hear from Ms. Alissa Wilson who is public education and advocacy coordinator for Africa for the American Friends Service Committee where she covers peace and security issues. Prior to this, she was researcher in Ethics and Human Development at Tufts, and an affiliate at the Global Equity Initiative at Harvard University.

Ms. Wilson has served as a long-term election observer with the National Democratic Institute in Nigeria and as a Jane Addams-Andrew Carnegie fellow at the Center on Philanthropy at Indiana University. She has conducted research at the U.N. and the Carter Center and facilitated peace education trainings in the U.S. and Nigeria.

We will then hear from Mr. Steve McDonald—again welcome back—who is currently the global fellow of the Woodrow Wilson International Center for Scholars, freelance writer, and international consultant. Until recently he was director of the Africa Program at the Wilson Center. He helped to design, initiate and manage the Wilson Center's leadership and building state capacity and post-conflict resolution programs in Burundi and other countries. A specialist in African affairs, Mr. McDonald has lived in and worked with Africa for 45 years and focused primarily on democracy and governance, human resource development, conflict resolution and transformation, peacebuilding, and policy formation for Africa.

Mr. Jobbins?

STATEMENT OF MR. MICHAEL JOBBINS, DIRECTOR OF GLOBAL AFFAIRS, SEARCH FOR COMMON GROUND

Mr. JOBBINS. Members of Congress, thank you so much for having us here and convening this meeting at a timely moment, and inviting us from the civil society groups who have been involved in Burundi over the years to join and share what we see happening in the country at this critical moment. I ask that my written testimony be entered into the record.

Mr. SMITH. Without objection, yours and all the distinguished witnesses, and any other materials you want to include.

Mr. JOBBINS. Thank you. The Search for Common Ground has worked in Burundi since 1995 to prevent violence and support social cohesion in the media, working with communities, and supporting dialogue processes. Today we support youth, religious, and community leaders to prevent violence on the ground, support radio programming with the stations that are broadcasting at the moment, and we continue to support efforts focused on land reform, youth and women's empowerment, and post-conflict education. I will begin by speaking briefly on recent developments, make three observations about the current crisis, and conclude with next steps.

Yesterday, Burundi held its Presidential elections. Search assembled a pool of 150 journalists from the media organizations able to report on voting throughout the country. While results are expected tomorrow, early signs are trickling in and President Nkurunziza is widely expected to win those elections.

They took place against the backdrop of a political crisis, which began on April 25, with the ruling nomination, as expected, of President Nkurunziza to run for a third term. That triggered protests, as you alluded to, from civil society and opposition parties who felt it was unconstitutional, violated the Arusha Agreement and was a betrayal of the process that ended the civil war.

While the constitutional court upheld Nkurunziza's candidacy, protests have continued. There was an attempted coup in mid-May, and serious fighting has unfolded in Bujumbura periodically over the last few weeks. Despite mediation attempts, the impasse continues and will continue after the elections. The crisis has caused an estimated 100 deaths so far, and more than 100,000 to flee into neighboring countries.

There are three critical things that we need to understand this situation right now. First, the underlying, most critical issue is maintaining the social compact that is enshrined in the Arusha Agreement. Beyond the words that were agreed to, Arusha laid the bedrock for political order that was based on dialogue, political inclusivity, and tolerance. The Constitution may have set out the rules for governing the country, but Arusha enshrined the social compact in the same way that the Magna Carta serves in the United Kingdom or the Declaration of Independence does here in America.

During the peace process, all parties committed to move beyond a sense of winner-takes-all politics and to build a Burundi where all Burundians could live in peace. That peace process forced a culture of dialogue and the question is now, after this polarization, can that social compact be restored? The answer will depend on the actions of the next government over the next few days as well as how bodies like the Land Commission, the Truth and Reconciliation Commission, and the Human Rights Commission handle some of the most contentious issues that will be put before it.

Second, we need to recognize what the crisis is not. Despite the political crisis, the Burundian people have put the ethnic dimension to the crisis behind them. The overwhelming majority of Burundians across the country reject violence, support tolerance, and want to see a consensus to end the crisis right now. The fact that ethnic identity has not played a role in the crisis is a testament to the Burundian people but also to the effectiveness of international cooperation.

It has been with USAID and State Department support that the interethnic reconciliation through people-to-people approaches has taken place. And it is with concerted effort from the U.S. and its international partners that the military integration was able to proceed so successfully. And if we haven't seen either an ethnic dimension to the crisis or the security forces splitting into interregional or identity factions is due in large part to the support that they have received.

Third, we have to remember that the crisis comes against one of the most desperate poverty situations in the world. Burundi is the size of Maryland with a population of 10 million and nearly everyone is a farmer. In some areas, the average farm yields enough food for just 3 months out of the year to feed a family. As a result it is one of the fastest urbanizing countries in the world, with young people moving to the cities with little future and little economic hope.

If you look at projections from IFPRI, the research center down the road, childhood malnutrition scenarios will drop from 45 percent to 40 percent over the next 35 years. You cannot have a situation with 40 percent malnutrition for the next 35 years without expecting a series of both political and humanitarian crises to continue to unfold. It is unthinkable that this situation can persist and that there can be a solution without international assistance both to the democratic governance consolidation in the country as well as to regional economic integration and growth.

The appointment of Tom Perriello as Special Envoy is an opportunity for the U.S. to play a positive role in the short- and long-term solutions, and thank you to the subcommittee for advocating strongly for that. At the same time, there is reason to hope that the talks will resume following these elections and that there can be confidence built between the different political factions operating the country right now.

But we have to remember that American attention to Burundi has historically lurched from one crisis to another. We talk about elections, we talk about democratic governance and justice now, but over the last 5 years the DG and justice budget was zero. USAID has not made Burundi one of its resiliency priorities and there hasn't been concerted accompaniment of economic integration in the region, even though it is one of the poorest countries, if not the poorest country in the world.

And so as I conclude my remarks, I just want to focus on the opportunity that we have for the U.S., with Perriello's leadership, to make a broad, strategic commitment to preventing the crises of today as well as the crises of tomorrow, and using all of the instruments that are available—development, cooperation, diplomatic engagement—to see through the Burundian people to a peaceful solution to this crisis. Thank you very much.

[The prepared statement of Mr. Jobbins follows:]

Written Testimony

by Mike Jobbins

Submitted to the

House Subcommittee on Africa, Global Health, Global Human Rights, and International Organizations

JULY 22nd 2015

Members of Congress, Ladies and Gentlemen:

Chairman Smith, Representative Bass, and Members of the Committee, I would like to begin by thanking you for convening this timely and important meeting, and for the chance to update you on the current situation in Burundi.

I thank the Committee for the leadership that it has shown in supporting peace in Burundi and for ensuring that American values of tolerance, fundamental freedoms, and democratic dialogue hold a key place in our foreign policy in Africa and the world. I would also like to recognize my co-panelists, Dr. Ndura, Mr. McDonald, and Ms. Wilson, who have each dedicated years to supporting peace in the country, and are among the most thoughtful analysts of Burundian affairs here in Washington.

My name is Mike Jobbins, I work on conflict transformation with Search for Common Ground, and served with Search in both Burundi and the DRC between 2008 and 2010. I have covered the country in one way or another since 2004, and was in Bujumbura in the run-up and during the outbreak of the current crisis. My testimony alludes to some of Search's work in the country, but the views expressed are my own. I will begin by speaking briefly on recent political developments in Burundi, some of the causes of the crisis which the country is currently facing, and then conclude by considering some practical steps to reduce risks and improve the situation.

By way of introduction, Search for Common Ground has worked in Burundi for more than two decades. Search began in 1995, and worked throughout the war, the peace process, and has continued into the democratic era. We continue to address both the immediate crisis and longer-term drivers of conflict, focusing on supporting media, dialogue processes and community actions that prevent violence and support inclusive development and decision-making in the country. In the past two decades, our work has contributed to the peace and reconciliation process, the return of refugees and resolution of land conflict, and the development of a vibrant media sector. The programming in Burundi is supported by a range of donors including USAID, the State Department and the US Institute of Peace, as well as the European Union, UN Agencies, European governments, as well as foundations and individual donors.

Amidst the current crisis, support social cohesion and prevent violence. Our main actions include supporting women, youth, religious, and community leaders to encourage non-violence, producing news programming via our flagship Studio Ijambo radio studio, while also continuing our longer-term work on land conflict, women's involvement in public life, and integrating conflict resolution education into the schools.

Update on yesterday's elections, and the broader political context. Yesterday, Burundi held presidential elections. In order to ensure objective and transparent coverage of the electoral process, Search assembled a pool of 156 journalists from six radio stations, as well as our own Studio Ijambo, and the Agence Burundaise de Presse to report on the voting process throughout the day.

Three of the eight candidates withdrew shortly before the elections, although their withdrawals were not accepted by the Elections Commission, citing the short turnaround time. The remaining candidates include the incumbent President Pierre Nkurunziza, opposition challenger Agathon Rwasa, as well as candidates from the UPRONA, FNL, and COPA parties, and Nkurunziza is in a strong position to be re-elected. While the tabulating process is still underway, I can report that:

- In general, election-day security was good in most of the country. In Bujumbura, there were heavy gunfire and grenade explosions in a number of neighborhoods on the eve of the elections. One incident was reported in the Nyakabiga area of Bujumbura, where the body of a member of the opposition MSD party was found triggering protests in that neighborhood.
- In terms of voter turnout, as of midday, reporters in Rutana and Ngozi were reporting large early turnout. While in most other provinces, voting got off to a relatively slow start. As of the time of drafting we are still compiling reports, so we do not have definitive in many provinces.
- Elections observation was spotty, after boycotts by many local and international observer bodies. The the UN's MENUB and East African Community observers were deployed in several population areas. I understand that the independent Amizero y'aburundi movement and UPRONA party have fielded a few observers, though not many. There have been several complaints of polling stations opening late in some areas, suspicions triggered by last-minute changes in polling staff, and other isolated, relatively minor incidents.

Political Crisis. The elections took place against the backdrop of a broader political crisis that has led to an estimated 100 deaths, more than a hundred thousand displaced, and a deep political impasse. On April 25th, the ruling CNDD-FDD nominated President Pierre Nkurunziza to run for a third term in office. His nomination triggered protests from civil society groups and opposition parties, who argued that a third term was unconstitutional and violated the Arusha Agreements, the initial peace deal that laid the groundwork for an end to Burundi's civil war. While the Constitutional Court upheld Nkurunziza's candidacy and noted that the Constitution's language was vaguer than the Arusha Agreement, protests intensified against the candidacy and electoral process.

Regional mediation efforts were disrupted by an attempted coup on May 13 which, though quickly put down, saw serious fighting in Bujumbura, the destruction and shuttering of many of the principal independent news media outlets, and a grave escalation to political crisis. The impasse has persisted, opposition groups have boycotted the electoral process, several UN-brokered dialogue processes have broken down and the most recent regional mediation attempt, led by Ugandan President Yoweri Museveni has not yet yielded a solution. At the same time, violence erupted two weekends ago with apparent insurgents clashing with security forces in northern Kayanza province, heavy firing was reported as recently as Monday night, and unconfirmed rumors of plots for armed struggle launched from outside the country continue.

Three Observations. I would like to make three general observations about the current conflict in Burundi, to help understand its causes and how its international partners, including the U.S., might best help to address it:

1. **A Backdrop of Desperation.** The current crisis comes amidst some of the most crippling poverty on earth. A country the size of Maryland, Burundi is home to more than 10 million people, nearly all of whom depend on farming for their livelihoods. Even with its rich volcanic soil, small plot sizes barely yield enough food for many families. According to USAID-funded research in 2010, 45% of children under five are anemic, and NGOs report stunting rates of 57%. A 2010 analysis by the Food and Agricultural Organization noted that in some parts of northern Burundi, the average smallholder farm could feed a family of five for just two or three months out of the year – the remaining nine months they were left to their own devices.

   In this context of rural desperation, it is no surprise that Burundi has had the third-highest rate of urbanization in the world, after only Qatar and its northern neighbor Rwanda. Many of the recent migrants to cities have been young, poor, with little hope for a better future. The future for young Burundians is even more challenging: projections by researchers the International Food Policy Research Institute, show that even under "optimistic" scenarios, childhood malnutrition will drop from 45% today to just under 40% by 2050.

   It is inconceivable that a 40% malnutrition rate in one of the poorest nations, rapidly urbanizing countries on the planet can persist for the next 35 years without further political crises. The current crisis is occurring against the backdrop of fundamentally broken mathematics. Without support to efforts at regional integration and a growth in non-farm income, it is difficult to imagine long-term peace and stability.

2. **What is at stake?** The debate around the current political crisis in Burundi has focused on the Arusha Agreements, which were signed 15 years ago, next month. The Arusha agreements set out a path to end the country's civil war, and laid the bedrock for the new political order. The postwar political order has been based upon the principles of dialogue, political inclusivity, and guarantees that Burundi could be the home of all Burundians, regardless of ethnicity, region, or politics. While the Constitution laid the groundwork for governing the country, the principles enshrined in Arusha reflect a broader social compact – similar to the Magna Carta in Great Britain or the Declaration of Independence here in the U.S. In that way, it has become more than the text itself, a reflection of the will of the Burundian people to move beyond winner-takes-all politics and exclusionist rule.

   It is because of that social compact that more than ten thousand families – many of whom did not even have enough land to feed themselves – accepted to share their land with returning refugees, in the service of the broader process of peace in the country. The reintegration of nearly 400,000 returning refugees into a land-poor and chronically malnourished country is a testament to the heroism of ordinary Burundians who sacrificed for peace. Within this context, Burundi developed one of the most vibrant environments for media and public discourse about ethnicity, politics, and the legacy of the war.

The fundamental question that the current crisis poses to all of Burundi's leaders, as well as their international partners, is less about who will make up the next government of Burundi, but whether the social compact that values the spirit of dialogue, national unity, and vibrant inclusive discourse that accompanied the end of the war can be preserved following the polarization that has come with the electoral crisis. It is that fundamental social compact that must be preserved and enshrined within the post-electoral system.

3. **What this crisis is not.** While thus far I have focused on what this crisis is, it is equally important to recognize what the crisis is not. The loss of life, the suffering of the displaced, and the anger and fear on display throughout the political crisis are unconscionable tragedies. At the same time, when I began learning about Burundi a decade ago, it would have been unthinkable that you would have a profound political crisis, urban demonstrations, and a coup attempt – and yet the crisis has not yet taken on the ethnic undertones that many had feared. When there was a coup attempt, the army remained largely unified in rejecting it, and throughout the crisis has been widely viewed as professional and apolitical.

The lesson that I draw from this is that "you get what you pay for." Burundian leaders and ordinary citizens devoted time, money, and self-sacrifice to ensuring that army integration was successful. Courageous men and women across Burundi, often with support from religious and community leaders, chose to put ethnicity behind them as a dividing line, and that remains as a bulwark for peace today. Army reform efforts were supported by a range of international partners, including the U.S., and Burundian-led interethnic reconciliation efforts, were also a focus of international assistance, including through people-to-people Conflict Management and Mitigation programs.

The fact that ethnic identity and the army have not been manipulated into driving violence in the current crisis on a large scale is first and foremost a testament to the courage and strength of the Burundian people to put the crisis behind them. Secondarily, it is a testament to the effectiveness of international support, without which the current crisis would very plausibly have been worse. At the same time, many of the current drivers to the crisis were specifically those that did not receive as much attention. There has been little sustained support to democratic governance and institution-building in the country, and little focus on the media sector as a whole. There has been little effort to meet the growing aspirations of a poor, and increasingly urban, youth population. The specific areas where there was not sustained attention have been those that have featured prominently.

Responding to the Current Crisis. While many observers focused on the risk of violence during the electoral process as the principle threat to peace and stability in the country, we see a need for continued US diplomatic and programmatic engagement over the years to come.

Short-Term. In the immediate post-electoral context, confidence-building measures will be critical to shore up the social compact. The appointment of Tom Perriello as Great Lakes Special Envoy represents a key opportunity for the United States to work closely with Burundi's neighbors to play a positive role and to continue to support regional efforts to broker a consensual solution to the ongoing crisis. While deep differences remain, as far as I can see, progress on several "low hanging fruits" can help build confidence from the different political actors. This includes the African Union offer of human rights observers to document the situation in the country, working with national leaders. The continued absence of news media that have been damaged and suspended since the coup crisis has created an opportunity for rumors and misinformation to flourish. While all sides have committed to seeing these media reopened, there is significant divergence on the legal process for reopening the stations; progress to ensuring greater access to information and public debate, while maintaining safeguards against hate speech, could be instrumental in decreasing tension.

Medium Term. The degree to which democratic dialogue continues after the elections, and to which the new government is inclusive of different political tendencies, and able to preserve a vibrant political debate will be critical to preserving the long-term social compact that has guided the country's long-term process of peace consolidation.

In that context, several key institutions will be critical, and likely to handle some of the most contentious issues. That includes the National Human Rights Commission, which appears to be the most likely body to address complaints emerging from the violence that we have seen over the past months. The Truth and Reconciliation Commission, established just before the electoral process, will be responsible for handling the contentious legacy of conflict in Burundi, and can go a long way towards addressing the legacy of a contentious past. Finally, the Land Commission, the CNTB, handles some of the most challenging and contentious cases. It was suspended several months ago, due to localized protests against its decisions, and the degree to which it can maintain the confidence of ordinary Burundians across the country to handle disputes transparently will be viewed by many at the grassroots level as a bellwether for the sustained commitment to addressing and resolving divisive issues in a consensual manner.

Long Term. As I said earlier, the underlying mathematics of the crisis in Burundi do not work, and it is difficult to imagine consolidating long-term peace without sustained commitment to international support and engagement. Even as we respond to the latest crisis, we need to address some of the underlying structural dynamics. Improving food security, and increasing opportunities for non-farm income are critical Burundi's long-term future. The latter of these challenges hinges on improved investments in an educational sector that gives Burundian students both technical knowledge and social skills to compete in a regional and global economy, support to regional integration, and improved economic governance. Additionally, Regional bodies, including the Economic Community of the Great Lakes Region, the Lake Tanganyika Authority, and the Ruzizi Power Pool, among others, can unlock opportunities for growth.

Finally, while the U.S. is rightfully focused on the current electoral crisis in the country, attention has waxed and waned over the years, lurching from crisis to crisis. Even as U.S. recalls the commitments that Burundians made in Arusha, it is not clear to me that the accompaniment by the United States was what we would have imagined when Bill Clinton went to Arusha to observe the signing 15 years ago. While policymakers are rightly concerned about the state of democratic governance in Burundi today, we have to recognize that for the last five years, the budget for Democratic Governance programming in the country was zero. Sustained diplomatic and development engagement is necessary to support the longer process of consolidating long-term peace in Burundi and supporting resiliency to chronic crises.

Mr. SMITH. Thank you so very much for your testimony and your recommendations.

Dr. Ndura?

STATEMENT OF ELAVIE NDURA, PH.D., PROFESSOR OF EDUCATION, GEORGE MASON UNIVERSITY

Ms. NDURA. Thank you. I am very grateful to be here. I am grateful for this initiative to get more information about Burundi in order to hopefully shape and frame policies and actions that will be able to help the Burundian people build a peaceful country and peaceful communities.

I was asked particularly to focus on ethnic relations in Burundi's struggle for sustainable peace. Just like my friend Mike, here, I request that my testimony be included in the official record.

Mr. SMITH. Without objection, so ordered.

Ms. NDURA. Thank you. Let me begin briefly by stating that I am quite honored to sit here as a Burundian woman, as a Hutu Burundian woman who was severely victimized by ethnic conflicts in Burundi as I was forced to leave a life of single motherhood, of a political asylee, an immigrant in the United States, thankfully, after my husband who was Hutu was assassinated by the Tutsi-dominated government.

So when I talk about ethnicity, it is real. It is real. I have focused my entire livelihood, my entire professional career on education in the hopes of contributing to the education and the supporting and the sustaining of a new generation that will be able to work together across ethnic lines to really engineer, co-engineer a sustainable future for Burundi and for the African Great Lakes Region.

In terms of background, the history of Burundi can be divided into four main stages, what I call phases. First, the pre-colonial era, because people always wonder what is this ethnicity thing? People are all the same in Burundi. They speak the same language. They have, really, very much the same culture.

So what is going on in Burundi? It is very difficult to understand. So many scholars agree that in the pre-colonial era ethnicity was there as a marker, but not as a major source of conflict. But during the colonial era, the Belgian colonialists in many ways divided the communities both in Burundi and in Rwanda, geographically and politically, and really very much created what we have come to know in academia and in daily life as Tutsi hegemony.

Education was made a privilege that mostly Tutsi aristocrats were able to access and that continued even after the independence that Burundi acquired in 1962 as the structures were never changed. Hutus who have always constituted the majority of the country, about 84 percent, while Tutsis as Mike mentioned are 14 percent, we also have a very small minority of Twa as some people call them the Pygmies. We have Twas in Burundi and DRC, Democratic Republic of the Congo, and in Rwanda. They are very much a forgotten and an underserved part of the population, and yet which has always been exploited by both the Tutsis and the Hutus, especially during the war because they have been given weapons and asked to fight on whichever behalf.

So this post-colonial era is itself divided in three phases: The 1962 to 1992, 1993 to 2005, 2005 to the current day in 2015. The first phase of the post-colonial era really continued, without interruption, the colonial divisions where the Tutsis were in charge, had control over the military, the economy, education. If you really wanted to get through any door during that time you had to have been connected to a Tutsi somehow. Some of us barely survived. I have more information in my most recent book, which opens with my story as a Hutu woman, for reference later.

Nineteen ninety three saw Burundi turning the corner and becoming, attempting at least to become a democratic country by holding Presidential elections, which for the first time had many parties that were represented, which led to the election of Melchior Ndadaye, the very first Hutu and civilian ever to become elected President of Burundi. Unfortunately, hardliners within the Tutsi military assassinated him after only 100 days in power, and that set off the killings and the civil war that lasted 12 years.

Let me back up first and mention that many in the international community including the United States, when they talk about genocide they always refer to the Rwandan killings of 1994. Very few people realize that in 1972, next door Burundi, also had a genocide, this time of the Hutus by the predominately Tutsi government and the military. So Rwanda and Burundi have always fed on each other's history and present all the time, so it is very, very difficult to tell them apart.

The third phase of the post-colonial era, which is why many of you are interested today, the 2005 to 2015, it is a period that has been framed in many ways by the Arusha Accords that everybody probably will be talking about here, because the Arusha Accords that got all the parties together, even civil society, the international community together, to create a framework that would allow Burundi to move forward not just as a democratic country, but as a diverse country, as a country where everybody was going to be able to have a voice, everybody was going to have opportunities open to them. And I believe that is what all the Burundian people, both within Burundi and outside of Burundi, were hoping for, here is the Arusha Accord, finally.

There is something that has happened in my research. I travel to Burundi a lot. My entire research agenda is dedicated to Burundi and the African Great Lakes Region. There is something good that has come out of the Arusha Accords—voice. The people of Burundi have reclaimed their voice. They speak up. The question that I ask then, do we listen when they speak up?

And I think that is my major contribution today, because in terms of moving forward for Burundi and in efforts to avoid the recurrence or renewed violence based on ethnicity or any other intergroup dynamics, voices, the voices of the people must be heard. So I propose that we, the Burundian people, the current government, the opposition, everybody get together in order to really hold some honest conversations. Conversations where people express themselves, but also are willing to listen.

I think my major concern ever since April of this year, my major concern has been the lack of spaces for those kinds of conversations. People have been saying many things. People have been talking. But as a researcher and a person who loves Burundi and has been invested in Burundi for many years, I have constantly been wondering if anyone is listening.

Is President Nkurunziza listening? Is the current government listening? What are they hearing when people say ''no'' to the third term bid? Is it just about the third term bid or is it something else that is complicating the current situation? But we cannot unearth all those reasons unless we listen with compassion. Listening with compassion, in my mind, means listening, knowing that everybody talks in good faith, and that is what I hope. But then that is a question. As a researcher, I have more questions than answers. So are all the people who are talking, talking in good faith? Do they have some kind of ulterior motives, something that they stand to gain or that they stand to lose?

Let us go back to ethnicity. Yes, the government is mixed. Yes, even the Imbonerakure, the renowned youth militia. In some strategic areas in Burundi even the Imbonerakure is ethnically mixed. So, when some people go to those mixed areas they don't talk about ethnicity. However, it has emerged that when they go to talk in the campaign in promoting agendas in places that do not have Tutsi members among the Imbonerakure, the conversation shifts to, ''Hey, remember.'' Remember you have to support us, otherwise the Tutsi will get you again.

So for me, I am sitting here confused and wondering, so where is Burundi? Is it really post-ethnic? I argue that Burundi is no more post-ethnic than the United States is post-racial. Ethnicity, even on the surface, we think that ethnicity, people have made peace with ethnicity. Tutsi, Hutu, Twa are ready to work together and move forward together. I consider it a neverending undercurrent, almost a convenient divider that can be brought in at any time to advance some kind of agendas, wherever the agendas are coming from.

So how do we deal with that then? I focus on the common good. When you walk into Burundi and travel across the country, one of the most striking things that you would notice is the major difference between people who have access to resources and people who have no access to resources. From big houses and big hotels and big cars and several employees in the house, to the villages where people have no food, where people have no shelter, where children walk around and run around in coats that have become so oversized and so brown because they can't even afford soap to wash them.

So where is Burundi going, and how is violence contributing to worsening the situation of the real Burundian people beyond the politicians, beyond the policymakers? That is a major question for us to ponder because that is where the work needs to be done.

Let us go back to education. I consider education to be a key path forward toward the reconstruction of the communities of Burundi, these communities that have been shattered by endless conflicts and violence. We do have the framework culturally. You know Ubuntu is not South African only. The ethic of Ubuntu is actually African. We have an author, Kayoya, who wrote a book and talked about Ubuntu the same way as Desmond Tutu framed Ubuntu for the future of South Africa. I propose that education be grounded again in those traditional mechanisms and philosophies that rekindle the spirit of interdependence that really has always defined the Burundian people and the Burundian communities.

Reflective citizenship. I propose that investments be made to build the capacity of the Burundian people, especially the youth, to become reflective citizens. Those citizens who don't only vote because they stand to gain from the one who wins, but the people who run for office because they are convinced that if they win, the livelihoods of the people in those poor villages will actually be improved. Otherwise, for me, it doesn't matter who wins and who loses. It really doesn't matter.

I guess you can tell that I don't stand here to gain anything. That is the beauty of being an academic. Tenured, too, so I can say what I want as long as it is constructive. So education for reflective citizenship. Education that promotes youth peaceful engagement and reflective citizenship. Burundian people love children. We sing to them all the time. We have amazing lullabies that even my grandsons adore. To go to sleep when they visit with me, they ask me to sing the lullaby which states how special they are and how loved they are and how we will always be there to protect them against the enemy.

How can we rekindle the spirit that treasures the youth through education instead of arming them as child soldiers, instead of arming them as militias who kill even one another, sometimes resorting to killing even their own relatives? For what purpose? To get some money, to get some food, to get some clothes.

So you are powerful policymakers and that is why I am trying to tell the truth here, because we cannot focus on Burundi as yet just another troubled and troublesome country and a region of the world where we cannot do anything. We can do something, but we have to be honest with ourselves and our policies. And, in fact, develop and implement policies that will actually empower the people of Burundi to change their livelihood from the roots, not at the surface.

When we go in to do peacebuilding we are already in trouble. They are fighting, so we need to go in. Yes, it is good to go in, but what if we were to say we are going in to start educating the Burundian people from the bottom, from the roots? From the grassroots, so that when they graduate from school, or even if they drop out from school they have the spirit of unity, they have the spirit of interdependence, they have the spirit of reflective citizenship, instead of thinking, when I graduate I want to be able to build the biggest hotel and charge the most money that I can. How can we change this kind of thinking so that we reconstruct the Burundians to say this? Thank you.

[The prepared statement of Ms. Ndura follows:]

Ethnic Relations and Burundi's Struggle for Sustainable Peace

Prepared for the 22 July 2015 U.S. House Foreign Affairs Committee Hearing on the Current Political Situation in Burundi

by

Dr. Elavie Ndura

Professor, George Mason University

Burundi's population is composed of three ethnic groups: Hutu (85 percent), Tutsi (14 percent) and Twa (1 percent). Ethnic relations have evolved and shifted throughout Burundi's history throughout the pre-colonial, colonial, post-colonial, and contemporary eras. Understanding the complexity underlying inter-ethnic co-existence is, therefore, essential to preventing the recurrence or intensification of inter-ethnic violence as Burundi negotiates the current electoral turmoil.

The Pre-Colonial Era

The pre-colonial Burundian people are considered to have been mostly a peaceful people. Ethnicity existed as a socio-cultural identity marker. But, due to intermarriages and other cross-cutting ties, ordinary Tutsi and Hutu were largely on equal social footing. This rendered Tutsi-Hutu distinctions on the basis of ethnicity, feudal power relations, or socioeconomic status difficult to make. One of the distinctive feature, although by no means exclusive, was occupation as Hutus were mostly farmers while Tutsi were mostly postoralists. Tutsis pastoralists established themselves as the dominant minority group or ruling elite. Yet, there was no widespread interethnic violence. Some historians posit that the potential for conflict between Hutu and Tutsi was contained by the existence of Ganwa, an intermediate princely class between the Mwami (King) and the population. Many scholars contend that racist Belgian colonial policies and practices crystalized Tutsi-Hutu ethnic borders, thus creating a context for polarized interethnic relationships.

The Colonial Era

Initially, German and later, Belgian colonial governments used "indirect rule" to govern what was then called Rwanda-Urundi. Both colonial governments, recognizing the feudal structure in place decided to govern Rwanda-Urundi through the existing traditional political structures of authority controlled by the minority Tutsi elites. Use of colonial indirect rule did nothing to erode or diminish minority Tutsi hegemony over the majority Hutus. Colonial rule, which lasted 68 years (1894-1962), bolstered/reinforced minority Tutsi dominance over the majority Hutu in both Rwanda and Burundi. Through indirect rule, the Belgian colonial government enabled the Tutsi minority in Burundi to retain control over political power and to enjoy great access to economic resources and opportunities. Sons of Tutsi aristocrats benefited extensively from the European-type educational opportunities made available through Catholic missionary schools. Once educated, the Tutsi elite filled in the top and middle level administrative positions in the Belgian colonial government. As a result, the Tutsi elite who were already dominant in the colonial administration were favored and promoted over the Hutus. Hence, Belgian colonial policies and practices constructed the Tutsi minority into an alien superior (ruling) Hamitic race, while the Hutu majority were constructed into an indigenous Bantu race, ruled by the Tutsi elite. Towards the end of their administration in the 1960s, the Belgians called for the creation of a representative plural society, which inevitably benefited the already well entrenched and advantaged Tutsi minority elite. Racist Belgian colonial policies and practices reshaped and transformed Tutsi and Hutu ethnic identities into highly politicized racial identities with great potential for violent conflict. During the Belgian colonial rule in Rwanda-Urundi, Tutsi-Hutu ethnic identities were transformed into bipolar racial identities with profound social and political consequences.

The First Post-Colonial Phase: 1962 to 1992

Since achieving political independence from Belgium in 1962, Burundi has consistently experienced cyclical interethnic conflict and violence, the most notable being the 1972 genocide of the Hutu by the Tutsi-dominated government and military. The ethnic hatred between the minority Tutsi and majority Hutu that emerged during the colonial era erupted in open conflict and violence in 1961, following the assassination of Prince Louis Rwagasore, leader of the UPRONA nationalist and royalist political party.

The rift within the Burundian aristocracy over Burundi's independence from Belgium occurred at the same time political parties were being created to prepare the country for self-government in 1961.

Burundi became independent first as a monarchy in 1962 (same year as Rwanda) and was proclaimed a republic in 1966. Unlike in Rwanda where Hutus came to power after independence in 1962 (following the 1959 social revolution), in Burundi the Tutsi were in power before and after colonial rule. However, the Hutu revolution in Rwanda provided the nascent Hutu elites of Burundi with the 'model polity' they tried to emulate later. On the other hand, it gave the incumbent Tutsi grounds for their incipient fears of Hutu majority domination. Indeed, the Tutsi in Burundi controlled political power and the military. The initial split within the Burundian aristocracy and political tensions created during the politics of independence (between 1960 and 1962), did not lead to Tutsi-Hutu violence or massacres as was the case in Rwanda in 1959. However, the split within the Burundi aristocracy and political competition between UPRONA and PDC (caused by the Belgian colonial administrations' manipulations) gave rise to the early political conflict between Tutsi and Hutu in Burundi.

The first explosive violence against Hutus came in October 1965, when a group of Hutu military officers staged an unsuccessful coup d'état directed at the Tutsi-dominated government. The mutineers took a big gamble and lost. And the losses far exceeded the revenge Tutsis exacted upon the Hutu community. In addition to exterminating the entire first generation of Hutu military officers and political leaders, "an estimated 5000 Hutu civilians lost their lives in the capital (of Bujumbura) alone at the hands of local civilian defense groups organized under the supervision of the [Tutsi] army and governor". The Burundi monarchy, once the rallying point for moderate Tutsis and Hutus, could no longer sustain the status quo or prevent the worsening relations between the two ethnic communities as its authority had been greatly eroded. As previously indicated, the weakened monarchy was overthrown in 1966 by then Prime Minister, Captain Michel Micombero, who proclaimed Burundi a republic with himself as president. From 1966 until 1972, President Micombero headed a new government proclaimed of 'Unity and Revolution'. Although Micombero's government included Hutu cabinet ministers, the government firmly remained in Tutsi hands, with Tutsi extremists holding key positions inside and outside the army. For some Hutu elites, the consequences of the failed 1965 coup attempt were clear. They realized that they had no alternative but to start an armed rebellion against Tutsi control of both the government and army.

In 1969, the Hutu tried another insurrection against Tutsi hegemony, but it failed with deadly consequences for the mutineers. According to Melady, "in the 1969 troubles, 67 Hutu leaders were accused of trying to overthrow the government; they were tried, and 26 were executed by firing squad in December 1969". Despite two failed attempted coups detat (in 1965 and 1969) with deadly consequences, "a majority Hutu uprising took place in 1972". In contrast to the two previous rebellions, the 1972 uprising was organized on a much broader and more violent scale. The former U.S. Ambassador to Burundi (1969-1972), Thomas Melady, described the 1972 Tutsi-Hutu strife as " . . . one of the worst bloodbaths of this century – and one of the least known". According to the U.S. Ambassador, "The severity of the Tutsi response was probably rooted in the fear that such a plot would result in the wholesale killing or expulsion of Tutsis". Indeed, it is reported that President Micombero and other Tutsi leaders felt there was a vast Hutu conspiracy to eliminate them once and for all.

Although the hatred and hostility on both sides was deep and personal, the "genocide by the Tutsi's against the Hutus in Burundi . . . exceeded in its horror the genocide by the Hutus against the Tutsis in Rwanda ten years earlier". The massacres of Hutu by Tutsi were not only related to the immediate strife, but also to revenge motivated by deep-rooted hatred of Hutu.

Stavenhagen has described the horror of the Tutsi massacres of the Hutus in Burundi in 1972 this way:

"Within hours of its outbreak, a reign of terror was unleashed by Hutu upon the Tutsi, and then on an even more appalling scale by Tutsi upon Hutu. The killings went on unabated for several months. By then almost every educated Hutu element was either dead or in exile. Some conservative estimates put the total number of [Hutu] lives lost at 100,000, others at 200,000. Approximately 150,000 Hutu refugees fled to neighboring territories. "

The crises that occurred in Burundi between 1965 and 1972 were decisive in intensifying Tutsi-Hutu hatred and violence. The U.S. Ambassador characterized the hatred between Tutsi and Hutu in Burundi in the early 1970s this way:

While the animosity between the Hutu and Tutsi communities [in Burundi] had been evident to me [Sic.] from the beginning, I had underestimated how deeply rooted it was, like a malignant growth, spreading through all their relationships.

Between 1972 and 1987, "only Tutsi elements were qualified to gain access to power, influence and wealth". In contrast, the Hutu were systematically excluded from the army, civil service, economy and higher education. As a result, the Hutu were increasingly reduced to the hopeless status of a vast underclass in their own country. In 1976, a military coup d'état brought Colonel Jean-Baptiste Bagaza (from the same Southern Bururi Province as Michel Micombero) to power. Although President Bagaza proclaimed a government of "National Unity", he "did little to alter the stranglehold of Tutsi elements" within the government and army.

For the next three years (1976 to 1979), Burundi "remained firmly under the control of a Supreme Military Council consisting of 30 officers, all of them Tutsi". And the UPRONA political party, once a moderate nationalist movement with its membership cutting across ethnic and regional lines, became a stronghold of Tutsi extremist interests. The regime of

Bagaza fell in 1987 after yet another military coup d'état led by Major Pierre Buyoya, a young Tutsi military officer from the south of the country. In 1988, Buyoya was faced with a significant Hutu rebellion in northeast Burundi. In the same year, a local incident of Tutsi abuse and impunity in a rural commune triggered an explosive Hutu violence directed at Tutsi supremacy. The incident inevitably provoked a confrontation with the Tutsi dominated army, with deadly consequences for the Hutu community. Stavenhagen observes that, "although the exact number of Hutu victims remains a matter of speculation, estimates suggest that 15,000 may not be too wide a mark."

It is reported that soon after the 1988 massacre, the Buyoya regime introduced several constitutional and political reforms including increasing the number of Hutu cabinet ministers from six to twelve and naming a Hutu Prime Minister. However, because these reforms lacked Tutsi support or Hutu trust, they had no impact on the Tutsi-Hutu relations. To underscore the ineffectiveness of the reforms on Tutsi-Hutu relations, "renewed killings occurred in November 1991, with an estimated 3,000 Hutu killed by [Tutsi] government troops."

For a period of thirty years after Burundi achieved political independence from Belgium (1962-1992), the minority Tutsi held political power and controlled the army. During the same period, Hutu were excluded from the control of power and reduced to a vast underclass. Repeated massacres over three decades led to thousands of Hutus killed or forced into neighboring countries as refugees. And educated Hutus in government, higher education or the military were either exterminated or exiled.

The Second Post-Colonial Phase: 1993 to 2005

This period is marked by a 12 year civil war primarily ethnic nature. As a result of the first free and fair elections in decades, held in June 1993, FRODEBU unseated the long ruling UPRONA government. Melchior Ndadaye, a Hutu, was elected president. He affirmed his strong commitment to eliminating Burundi's "ethnic virus" and formed a government composed of one third Tutsi and a Tutsi Prime Minister. Despite this commitment, three months after his inauguration, the Tutsi military staged an attempted coup d'état that led to the assassination of President Ndadaye, the speaker of the National Assembly and several senior Hutu members of the FRODEBU government. Ndadaye's assassination unleashed massive anger among Hutu populations against Tutsis across Burundi, which was met with unselective reprisal and killings of Hutus by the Tutsi military. Hundreds of thousands, both Hutus and Tutsi, perished during the civil war.

An internal peace process which started in June 1998 prepared ground for the signing of the Arusha Peace Agreement in August 2000. Though both events were considered major political breakthroughs, ethnic violence persisted and many issues remained unresolved. The historic Arusha Peace Agreement was signed by nineteen political organizations and movements

The Third Post-Colonial Phase: Pierre Nkurunziza's Government and Uneasy Interethnic Partnerships (2005 to 2015)

Burundi's cyclical interethnic conflicts and violence are the result of decades of struggles between Tutsi and Hutu over political power and economic control. The smallest ethnic minority, the Twa, have mostly remained isolated and exploited by both the Hutus and Tutsi.

The struggles have occurred within the context of Tutsi dominance, political repression and economic deprivation of the Hutu majority.

The third post-colonial phase is characterized by interethnic collaboration, mostly as a result of the political framework that was created by the Arusha Peace Agreement. The Agreement established a power-sharing structure, which in turn helped to shape Burundi's new constitution. Power-sharing could foster interethnic peaceful coexistence, which was the underlying spirit of the Arusha Peace Agreement. However, a number of questions can be raised about the nature, scope, and motives of interethnic partnerships formed this phase. To what extent are interethnic partnerships grounded in shared visions for improving the wellbeing of all Burundian people? In what ways do personal motivations weaken the potential for meaningful and transformative interethnic partnership? How can healthy interethnic partnerships be sustained in a context that lacks spaces for courageous interethnic conversations about the past, present, and future?

Moving Forward: Preventing Interethnic Violence

Over the years, concerted efforts by internal and external actors to construct political solutions to the ethnic problem in Burundi have been largely undermined by deep rooted hatred and distrust compounded by mutual fears of annihilation on both sides of the conflict, which are further exacerbated by a culture of impunity. Additionally, the lack of shared national visions of societal reconstruction will continue to fuel the undercurrent of ethnic conflict and violence in Burundi. The negotiations and political compromises upon which national decisions are made have so far failed to take into consideration the fractured social fiber of the country, and instead focused on individual, even egotistical gains and benefits with little concern for the general population and the countless families that have been victimized by the decades long cycle of interethnic conflict and violence.

Therefore, for Burundi to avoid continued or renewed interethnic violence, people from all ethnic groups must develop their consciousness of the critical role that individuals and groups must play in the peacebuilding and social reconstruction processes in their nation. To this effect, opportunities must be afforded the people to share their narratives of war to facilitate mutual understanding and compassion for one another, thus empowering them to understand the critical nature of their civic responsibilities towards fostering social cohesion.

Hence, the following concrete recommendations are articulated to help prevent or curb further interethnic violence.

First, the intergroup openness and honesty that led to the articulation of the historic Arusha Agreement must be sustained among all Burundians and across all development sectors to create and sustain a society grounded in sharing and collaboration and defined by the common good. Second, a focus on the common good should inspire and shape people-centered reforms in all sectors to help reduce the growing gap between the elite, particularly government officials, and the masses. If left uncontrolled and untamed, the growing economic disparities will jeopardize the country's quest for peace. Third, leaders of the various political parties must critically reflect on their motivations and articulate national visions that transcend individual benefits so that they can best serve the people of Burundi. In the absence of this re-envisioning, individual interests will continue to blind stakeholders and fuel intergroup conflicts.

Fourth, education is a key path forward towards the reconstruction of communities that are united through shared principles and practices of Ubuntu. For this purpose, moving forward

21

implies empowering the youth to become reflective citizens. In this context, reflective citizenship is to be understood as "the re-examination, deconstruction, and unlearning of the hegemonic discourse of dominance and oppression that pervades our individual and collective lived experiences and dispositions. It is about understanding that as human beings, we are all forever bound in a destiny that only we can define"(Ndura, 2006, p.199).

Fifth, to frame and lead the way forward through education that promotes youth peaceful engagement and reflective citizenship, teacher education curriculum reform is needed to develop educators' capacity to practice peace pedagogy across all subject areas at all levels. Therefore, educators' professional development must be grounded in Ubuntu and social responsibility frameworks, and focus on constructive reflection; instructional materials evaluation, adaptation and development; student-centered pedagogy; conflict resolution; and community engagement (Ndura & Mimuraba, 2013).

Henceforth, context-grounded social realities in theory, policy and practice across curricula must drive the missions and goals of all education, teacher education and professional development programs.

References

Chrétien, J.P. (2003). *The great lakes of Africa: Two thousand years of history.* New York:

Zone Books.

Chrétien, J.P. (1985). Hutu and Tutsi au Rwanda et au Burundi. In J. L. Amselle & E.

M'Bokolo (Eds.), *Aur cœur de l'éthnie, tribalisme et état en Afrique.* Paris : Editions la Découverte.

Eller, J. D. (1999). *From culture to ethnicity to conflict: An anthropological perspective on international ethnic conflict.* Ann Arbor: The University of Michigan Press.

Kayoya, M. (2007). *Entre deux mondes: D'une génération à l'autre.* Bologna : Grafiche Universal.

Lemarchand, R. (2004).The Burundi genocide. In S. Totten, W. S. Parsons, & I. W.

Charny (Eds.), Century of genocide: Critical essays and eyewitness accounts (2nd ed.) (pp.321-337). New York: Routledge.

Lemarchand, R. (1994). *Burundi: Ethnocide as discourse and practice.* New York: Woodrow

Wilson Center Press.

Lemarchand, R. (1970). Rwanda and Burundi. London: Pall Mall Press.

Mahmood M. (2001). *When Victims Become Killers: Colonialism, Nativism, and the Genocide in Rwanda.* Princeton: Princeton University Press.

Makoba, J. W. & Ndura, E. (2006). The roots of contemporary ethnic conflict and violence in Burundi. In S. C. Santosh (Ed.), *Perspectives on contemporary ethnic conflict: Primal violence or the politics of conviction?* (pp. 295-310). Lanham: Lexington Books.

Melady, T. P. (1974). Burundi: The tragic years. Maryknoll, NY: Orbis Books.

Ndura, E. (2013). Fostering a culture of nonviolence through multicultural education. In R. Amster & E. Ndura (Eds.*). Exploring the power of nonviolence: Peace, politics, and practice (*pp. 206-218). Syracuse, NY: Syracuse University Press.

Ndura, E. (2011). Building a foundation for sustainable peace in Burundi: A transformative multicultural education approach. In E. Ndura, M. Meyer, & J. Atiri (Eds.), *Seeds bearing fruit: Pan-African peace action for the 21st century (pp.3-18).* Trenton, NJ: Africa World Press.

Ndura, E. (2006). Transcending the majority rights and minority protection dichotomy through multicultural reflective citizenship in the African Great Lakes region. *Intercultural Education,* 17(2), 195-205.

Ndura, E. & Nimuraba, S. V. (2013). Educating for democracy and social justice to further Burundi's 2025 Vision. *Procedia-Social and Behavioral Sciences,* 93, 714-718. Available at http://www.sciencedirect.com/science/journal/18770428/93

Ndura, E., Bangayimbaga, A. & Bandeba, V. (2012). Reclaiming Ubuntu through multicultural education: A foundation for peacemaking in the African Great Lakes region. In S.A. Nan, Z.C. Mampilly & A. Bartoli (Eds.) (pp. 295-307). *Peacemaking: From practice to theory.* Santa Barbara: Praeger.

Reyntjens, R. (1995). *Burundi: Breaking the Cycle of Violence.* In Minority Rights Group. Manchester, United Kingdom: Manchester Free Press.

Timpson, W., Ndura, E., & Bangayimbaga, A. (2015). *Conflict, reconciliation and peace education: Moving Burundi toward a sustainable future.* New York: Routledge/Taylor & Francis Group.

Mr. SMITH. Thank you very much, Dr. Ndura. Despite your personal loss, and again let me convey on behalf of our committee our condolences because I am sure that has to be an ever-present source of agony for you, but despite all that you continue to fight hard for a durable peace and reconciliation with an emphasis on education. So thank you for sharing and the history as well, which I thought was very fascinating.

Ms. Wilson?

STATEMENT OF MS. ALISSA WILSON, PUBLIC EDUCATION AND ADVOCACY COORDINATOR FOR AFRICA, AMERICAN FRIENDS SERVICE COMMITTEE

Ms. WILSON. Thank you. Thank you to Chairman Smith, Ranking Member Bass, and the members of this subcommittee for holding this important hearing. My name is Alissa Wilson, and as you have heard I serve as the public education and advocacy coordinator for Africa with the American Friends Service Committee, or AFSC.

The AFSC is a Quaker organization working in 56 locations throughout the world. Founded almost 100 years ago, we promote lasting peace with justice as a practical expression of faith in action. We were co-awarded the Nobel Peace Prize on behalf of all Friends in 1947, and have worked in Africa for over 50 years.

AFSC has worked in Burundi for over a decade, and like many Quakers before us we work with the belief that there is that of God in everyone. We have brought together people across lines of identity, ethnicity, religion, gender, and experience during war to heal and restore bonds of community. Our work with Burundian partners has yielded strong examples of communities resolving differences through inclusive dialogue and increasing self-reliance through livelihood approaches. We have also engaged actors at the sociopolitical level, on dialogue and exchange programs and on peacebuilding issues such as the Truth and Reconciliation Commission design and implementation.

Currently, the AFSC is supporting the Friends Church of Burundi on an emergency response project that has brought together leaders from different faith communities. At the local level, pastors, imams, and priests are encouraging congregations to take action for peace. These congregations come from all over the country and represent an array of political backgrounds. And at the national level, a small committee of religious body representatives will reach out to different sociopolitical actors to advocate for dialogue.

Our decade of experience working in Burundi leads us to three recommendations. First, help to revitalize the mediation process. Second, create a long-term U.S. strategy for Burundi that includes sustained funding for peacebuilding, democracy, rights, and governance programs. And finally, support regional actors in contributing to peace. Revitalizing the mediation process needs to be the top priority for the U.S. and other donors to help Burundi move past this very real crisis.

We welcome the appointment of Special Envoy Tom Perriello, the Special Envoy for the Great Lakes Region of Africa. We hope he will support increased coherence to the mediation process by coordinating with the mediation team, East African Community, African Union, and other key actors. Attention should also be paid to civil society at this moment. A range of nonpolitical Burundian organizations has been working on trust building and good governance issues since the Arusha Peace Agreement. They should be consulted by the mediation team and be included in post-mediation planning. Their inclusion makes these processes more accountable to citizens and strengthens transparency and credibility. We recognize that civil society participation should be negotiated with all actors to ensure that their ideas have a voice balanced appropriately with the role of political actors.

The Atrocity Prevention Board is to be commended for ensuring U.S. attention to Burundi over a year ago. However, an engagement strategy with Burundi should focus on long-term engagement not flashpoint prevention. Sustainable peacebuilding and development progress happens in the daily work between elections. And as Mr. Jobbins mentioned, democracy, rights, and governance funding for Burundi needs to increase. If we maintain these funding levels and continue to provide military assistance at significantly higher levels, what message are we sending to the people of Burundi?

An investment in long-term accounts shouldn't come at the expense of those for crisis prevention and response like the Conflicts Crisis Fund, or CCF. Flexible funds for unexpected challenges are still important. Unfortunately, for Fiscal Year 2016, for the second year in a row, the House budget did not allocate money for the CCF. The Senate passed a budget that included CCF but with only $30 million to cover efforts worldwide.

Finally, the history of the Great Lakes Region includes conflicts that have spilled across borders. Countries have also provided support or safe harbor to armed groups from their neighbors, and we urge the U.S. to use good offices with Burundi's neighbors to create a setting where each country supports peace processes and refrains from involvement in armed activities within or across borders. We also encourage the U.S. to remain committed to collaboration with the EAC, AU, U.N. and others to respond with rapid, high-level diplomatic engagement in case of heightened violence.

AFSC has worked in contexts of conflict across the globe for nearly 100 years and we understand that there is rarely an arrival in peacebuilding processes, there are cycles of challenges and opportunities for breakthrough. At this moment, Burundi once again faces a very real choice between reignition of conflict or a recommitment to building and maintaining sustainable peace and development. Regional actors, the U.S., and the global community at large must do all we can at this time to support the conditions for the latter to win the day. Thank you.

[The prepared statement of Ms. Wilson follows:]

American Friends
Service Committee

Office of Public Policy and Advocacy · 1822 R Street NW · Washington, DC 20009 · (202) 483-5370

Statement by
Alissa Wilson
Public Education and Advocacy Coordinator for Africa
American Friends Service Committee

Testimony before the U.S. House Foreign Affairs
Subcommittee on Africa, Global Health, Global Human Rights and International Organizations

Hearing: The Unfolding Crisis in Burundi
July 22, 2015

The American Friends Service Committee thanks Chairman Chris Smith, Ranking Member Karen Bass and the distinguished members of this subcommittee for holding this important hearing today.

The American Friends Service Committee is a Quaker organization working in 56 locations throughout the world, promoting lasting peace with justice as a practical expression of faith in action. Founded in 1917, AFSC has worked throughout the world in conflict zones, in areas affected by natural disasters, and in oppressed communities to address the root causes of war and violence; AFSC was co-awarded the Nobel Peace Prize for this work in 1947 on behalf of all Friends. AFSC has sought to address a wide range of challenges impacting countries in Africa for over 50 years - supporting efforts to end Apartheid in South Africa, healing the wounds of war in Mozambique, and establishing sustainable livelihoods for youth in Somalia, among many other initiatives. Today AFSC works in four countries in Africa - Zimbabwe, Somalia, Kenya and Burundi - and demonstrates the power of every community to solve its own problems creatively and nonviolently.

The Crisis Unfolding in Burundi

Emerging from a brutal civil war at the turn of the millennium Burundi has largely been hailed as a peacebuilding success story in the fifteen years since the Arusha Peace Agreement was signed. A deep citizen commitment to restoring broken bonds throughout society has helped bring the country forward, and nationwide reconciliation processes were beginning to take shape.

In recent months, disagreements among political actors over differing interpretations of the mandate of the President under the Arusha Peace Agreement and the national constitution have strained the fragile peace to which all actors have contributed in Burundi. The ruling party asserts that the current President has been in office for just one term through universal suffrage, while the opposition asserts that he has been in office for two terms. According to the opposition, another term in office would violate the Arusha Peace Agreement and constitution.

This disagreement has sparked a series of demonstrations since the 26th of April 2015 as reported in the international media. In the intervening period, over 140,000 people have fled the country, according to the UNHCR. They have fled due to violence, the fear of violence, and/or concern that they won't be able to provide for their families due to Burundi's flagging economy. As tensions have flared in this country where memories of civil war remain fresh, reports show that many have died from the violence, many others have been injured and there have been a substantive number of detentions.

The international community has responded to these developments in a number of ways, including the offer of mediators for a dialogue process. Unfortunately, two different mediators have been dismissed by the political dialogue's stakeholders, and the process has yet to yield a comprehensive agreement. There was an increase of violence in the wake of the parliamentary elections held on June 29th and there are concerns about what will happen in the post-electoral period after scheduled presidential elections this week.

AFSC's Work in Burundi

For over a decade, AFSC has carried out programs in Burundi on peacebuilding and conflict prevention, including initiatives to support community livelihoods, trauma healing, and national reconciliation. We have worked with women's associations, youth associations and others with a deep commitment to Burundi. We have also worked in partnership with Quakers in Burundi who, over the last 20 years, have developed a reputation for undertaking effective initiatives in community healing, community reconciliation and violence prevention. Rooted in the Quaker belief that there is that of God in every person, we have brought people together across lines of identity – ethnicity, religion, gender, and experience during war - to heal and restore bonds of community.

AFSC's work has engaged key actors at both the community and socio-political level. Our initial work at the socio-political level has led to an environment where we are able to organize dialogue and exchange programs that bring Burundian actors together with those from other countries in the global South. These programs focus on a number of different issues such as truth and reconciliation commission design and implementation, preventing election violence, etc. These programs have shown us the constructive opportunities that exist for working with national actors on issues that are critical to peace and nation-building.

The work we have done in Burundi has yielded strong examples of communities resolving their differences through inclusive dialogue and increasing self-reliance through community livelihood approaches. We have seen measurable success in the difficult, long-term work of reknitting a more healthy social and economic fabric within this nation in the wake of serious conflicts and challenges. These results have informed our understanding of the power of Burundian organizations and government institutions working at the community and socio-political levels.

In the current crisis, AFSC has supported religious leadership who wanted to work on peacebuilding activities. Before being a political being, everyone is a believer who belongs to a faith community that has some influence in their life. The important role of the faith community has also been recognized by Search for Common Ground, which has worked with faith leaders and with whom we partnered at the early stage of this program.

AFSC is supporting the Evangelical Friends Church of Burundi on an emergency response project which has brought together leadership from different faith communities to envision what they could do to support peace. At the local level, pastors, imams and priests are encouraging actions toward peace in congregations around the country, which include a diverse array of communities and political backgrounds. They are distributing messages of peace and encouraging dialogue with their members during both ecumenical services and out of church encounters. At the national level they have chosen a small committee of representatives from religious bodies to reach out to different socio-political actors working to advocate for peace and dialogue. It is hoped that through this emergency project, Burundians will agree to put aside their differences and work for the common good of the country.

Based on our work, we hope that the U.S. and international community engages government or political level actors as well as groups at the community level in efforts to forge durable peace, both now and into the future.

Recommendations for the USG and International Community

Others testifying today will discuss the issue of the third term, which certainly sparked the current crisis. However, our decade of experience working in this context leads us to urge the U.S. government to also focus on additional actions to diffuse the immediate crisis, and create a strategy for long-term engagement that supports the conditions necessary for sustainable peace.

Revitalize the Mediation Process

Revitalizing the mediation process should be a top priority for the U.S. and other governments in order to help Burundi move past this crisis. The international community needs to collaborate on a process with trust-building mechanisms that will enable actors to stay engaged and support complementary efforts for peace which are taking place in Burundian society. We welcome the appointment of the new U.S. Special Envoy for the Great Lakes, Tom Perriello. We hope that he will be able to support increased coherence within the mediation process by coordinating with the mediation team, East African Community (EAC), African Union (AU) and others working to support an end to the crisis. In the end, however, success depends on Burundian parties themselves being led by a spirit of concern for the well-being of the country and committing to good faith participation in the process.

The peace that has existed for a decade in Burundi has been based upon a conscious choice among the majority of Burundians to work toward reconciliation at individual and community levels. It is essential that these advocates for reconciliation are recognized and included in conversations about Burundi's future as much as those in conflict over what shape it should take. It is important to begin that engagement process now. We hope this is something the U.S. can support.

A range of Burundian organizations outside the political milieu have been working to support peace and good governance issues since the Arusha Peace Agreement. These impartial civil society organizations should be included in the mediation and post mediation planning processes, so that these processes benefit from their long-term experience and work on the issues underlying and beyond the current crisis. Involvement of these organizations will help produce results that benefit Burundian citizens and make the processes more accountable to them. It will also strengthen transparency and credibility. The shape or form of civil society participation in the mediation process should be negotiated with all actors to ensure that their ideas have a voice balanced appropriately with the role of political actors.

Burundian organizations that could play a supportive role in the current mediation process include those that have worked on trust building with a spectrum of groups including multiple political parties, the army, the police, ex-combatants, civil society and local leaders who are not politicians. The mediation team should consult Burundian organizations such as those that were involved with the work of Howard Wolpe, former U.S. Special Envoy to the Africa Great Lakes region, since they could bring institutional knowledge to the process based on their experiences after the Arusha Peace Agreement.

Depending on the nature of the mediation as it develops and what it covers, there will be a need to ensure that the perspectives of the Burundian public are also taken into consideration. This may necessitate complementary processes. Some issues that have come up during the crisis need to be separated from the major negotiation process, such as the revitalization of independent media.

Invest in Long-term Strategies

Long-term Strategies Not Flashpoint Prevention

The Atrocity Prevention Board's focus on Burundi, beginning over a year ago, is to be commended for ensuring U.S. government attention to conflict prevention. But the trends in approach and funding for prevention and peacebuilding need to move toward long-term strategies that recognize the cyclical, iterative nature of peacebuilding.

Burundi and other post-conflict countries traditionally receive little funding for peacebuilding and development in the years between elections. Too often, funding and programming are focused on the short period before a potential flashpoint. However, long term sustainable progress happens in the daily work that takes place over significantly longer periods of time. Support for a sustained and durable peace in Burundi will take dedicated time and investment beyond the immediate crisis. The need for such a strategy only intensifies if broader violence ensues during this period.

Burundian organizations with deep community experience can play an important role in generating ideas to advance and support long-term international community peacebuilding and development strategies, as they have in the past. In 2006, organizations instituted a process to generate ideas for Burundi's official collaboration with the UN peacebuilding structures (Peacebuilding Commission, Peacebuilding Support Office and the Peacebuilding Fund). These organizations put aside any political differences to develop suggestions for the years ahead, which were submitted to the government and subsequently included in official peacebuilding and development processes of the country.

U.S. investment in Burundi will find many willing partners for longer term engagement. The processes and institutions that create conditions for peace don't make the news the way those building toward conflict do; however, there are organizations throughout Burundi that have done incredible work to build social cohesion over time. They are the livelihoods organizations, like those that have put together micro-lending programs and savings circles that support groups with Hutu, Tutsi, Twa, returnees, ex-combatants, IDPs and women participants. They are the groups of young people coming together from across political party affiliations to create a better economic future for themselves. They are the religious leaders currently appealing for peace, helping to dispel rumors at the local level and keeping communities unified in working toward peaceful coexistence.

Funding for Democracy, Rights & Governance

AFSC does not accept USG funds for international work. However, we do track USG expenditures on the issues we care about. We note that there have been drastic cuts to core U.S. accounts that support democracy, rights and governance programs over the past few years. These cuts have directly impacted U.S. capacities to support long-term work needed to avert this and other crises.

Investing early to prevent conflicts from escalating into violent crises is, on average, 60 times more cost effective than intervening after violence erupts, according to research from the Carnegie Commission on Preventing Deadly Conflict. The current funding patterns for democracy, rights and governance ensure minimal availability of funds and no sustained funding beyond immediate crisis points. If we continue these funding levels and continue to provide military assistance to Burundi at much, much higher levels, what message are we are sending to the people of Burundi? Congress needs to increase funding for democracy, rights, governance and peacebuilding accounts. It also needs to signal to the Administration that it supports long-term investment for post-conflict countries, rather than continuing limited support around potential flashpoints.

Maintenance of Crisis Prevention and Response Accounts
There have also been challenges to funding more short term conflict prevention accounts. For FY2016, for the second year in a row, the House voted not to allocate any money for the Complex Crisis Fund (CCF). This account is currently funding violence prevention programs with youth in Burundi that are an important component in the APB's prevention efforts. The Senate has passed a version of the budget with $30M for CCF in total, for all its efforts across the globe.

U.S. Diplomatic Leadership
The U.S. embassy in Burundi has a small staff that is working diligently but they will need more colleagues if we ask them to increase activities. Additionally, as international support moves forward for Burundi, international donors will need to increase efforts to spend time outside Bujumbura to monitor and make necessary changes to their strategy of engagement. These trips will be important to ensure effectiveness and attenuate perceptions that the international community bases its ideas on the opinions of the cosmopolitan elite.

We hope that during the crisis, the U.S. embassy remains open to be able to engage in diplomatic activities. It is worth noting that, in general, the ability of U.S. diplomats and USAID staff to engage local communities in the post-Benghazi environment is very challenging. We urge Congress to weigh in on this issue with State Department Diplomatic Security to help clear the way for our vanguard of diplomacy and development to significantly engage with the communities where they are based.

Take a Regional Approach

The history of the Great Lakes region includes a range of significant conflicts that have spilled from one country to another. It also includes dynamics where countries have provided support or safe harbor to armed groups from their neighbors. There have been instances in the current crisis where either individuals or groups have expressed the desire to use force to take power. Nothing can be as important as fostering dialogue and working against violence, which would have repercussions for both Burundi and the entire region. We urge the U.S. to use its good offices with all of Burundi's neighbors to promote a setting where each country supports peace processes and refrains from getting involved in armed activities of any kind, within or across borders.

We also encourage the U.S. to remain committed to participation in regional approaches for coordination of diplomatic rapid response that could be helpful, particularly if violence breaks out. We hope that the U.S. collaboration with the EAC, AU, UN and others includes standing ready to respond with rapid and high-level diplomatic engagement in case of heightened violence.

Conclusion

The future of Burundi lies in the hands of Burundians – but the international community can provide important support for positive developments. Progress can be made if we invest in Burundi and make an effort to support the work of those committed to peace and development by engaging in the following activities:

Revitalize the mediation process in order to help Burundi move past this crisis

- The international community needs to collaborate on a process with trust-building mechanisms that will enable actors to stay engaged and support complementary efforts for peace which are taking place in Burundian society.
- Trusted Burundian organizations that have been working to support peace and good governance should be included in the mediation and post mediation planning processes, so that these processes might benefit from their long-term experience and work on the issues underlying and beyond the current crisis.

Create a strategy for long term engagement with Burundi that recognizes sustainable and durable peace and development will take dedicated time and investment beyond the immediate crisis

- Congress should increase funding for the core U.S. accounts that support democracy, rights and governance programs, which have been cut in recent years and now face further cuts. It should also signal to the Administration that investment needs to be made in long-term support to post-conflict countries, rather than continuing a limited focus on short term flashpoints.

Take a regional approach to the crisis that recognizes both potential spoilers and diplomatic rapid response

- The U.S. needs to use its good offices with all of Burundi's neighbors to ask them to support peace processes and refrain from getting involved in armed activities of any kind, within or across borders.
- The U.S. must remain committed to participation in regional diplomatic initiatives and stand ready to respond with rapid and high-level diplomatic engagement in case of heightened violence.

AFSC and Friends organizations from Kenya to Norway released a joint statement asking all Burundian actors to work for peace. AFSC commends the efforts of members of Burundian society and the international community who have ceaselessly supported peace in these difficult moments. We ask that you join us in continuing to hold Burundi in the Light.

There is rarely an "arrival" in peacebuilding processes - there are cycles that include ongoing challenges and opportunities for breakthrough. At this time Burundi once again faces a stark choice between re-igniting conflict or recommitting to the hard work of building and maintaining a sustainable peace. Regional actors, the U.S., and the global community at large must do all we can at this time to support the conditions for the latter option to win the day.

Thank you for providing me the opportunity to speak with the Committee today.

Mr. SMITH. Thank you so much, Ms. Wilson.
Mr. McDonald?

STATEMENT OF MR. STEVE MCDONALD, GLOBAL FELLOW, WOODROW WILSON INTERNATIONAL CENTER FOR SCHOLARS

Mr. McDONALD. Thank you very much for inviting me to testify today, Congressman Smith, and thank you very much for your warm remarks, welcoming remarks, Congresswoman Bass and Congressman Donovan. I appreciate the opportunity.

Batting cleanup is sometimes a disadvantage, sometimes an advantage because it allows me maybe to pick up on some points that I might have noticed that were not emphasized as much as I thought they should be. I was very involved in Burundi in 1993–94 during the election period then, and from 2002 to 2008 with a former colleague of yours, Howard Wolpe, one of your predecessors, Mr. Smith, in doing exactly the kind of work we have been talking about here in terms of reconciliation, trust building, capacity building amongst the key leaders of the country including working with the integration of the armed services there, the newly formed national army coming from the former armed rebel groups and the existing National Army.

We had quite a measure of success at that time working through the 2005 elections and the ceasefire in 2004 through the 2005 elections and beyond in terms of the demobilization, disarmament, and reintegration process. I mention this not to burnish my credibility but because it has been done. The kinds of things that my colleagues, particularly Alissa and Elavie and Mike, have referred to in terms of getting involved in long-term ways with democracy and governance and trust building, capacity building, education work has worked in the past. It is important to know that the crisis that we are facing now is a real one, but it is not ethnic in nature at this point, but it could become.

The basic rivalry here is a political one. The basic rivalry is a Hutu-Hutu rivalry as a matter of fact. The primary opposition members who are challenging Nkurunziza and challenging the third term issue are Hutu. That doesn't mean the crisis can't grow and take us back to the days of old and pick up on that underlying ethnicity consciousness that Elavie was referring to, which is certainly there, and therefore we have to be very, very conscious of not letting it get to that point. And I am glad to see that the United Nations, the African Union, the East African Community, and the United States have realized this and made statements to this effect.

The elections of course that we have just finished, we will know something about the results hopefully tomorrow. The elections commission in Burundi is saying that we had a 74 percent turnout. I personally think that is probably a very high figure, probably higher in the countryside than it was in Bujumbura. The feedback I am getting from people I know is that this is an exaggerated figure. We will see.

But the point is that the election has occurred. The opposition members who boycotted the election, although three of their names remained on the ballot, are now speaking out of a possibility of a unity government. I think that is a possibility that we should investigate, stay conscious of, that there may be still strands of dialogue and unity that we can bring together. You are all aware of course of the effort initiated by President Museveni to start a dialogue amongst the parties, again very late in the game. This was commendable but failed at the time, but there is no reason why that can't be picked up.

But another thing that is very important to realize is that the third term issue, the political issue that set this off, was only a trigger for the violence. As I think Mike was outlining for us, there are much, much deeper issues here. As we know, the country is extremely poor. Eighty percent of the population live in poverty, $420 a year GDP, soaring inflation.

I don't know if you are even aware that there were in July, early July and earlier in the year, protests around petrol and food prices and et cetera, and a strike was actually called at one point in time. The unemployment rate is 40 percent, much higher amongst the youth. Youth issues are extremely important. Malnutrition rates are very high. Chronic malnutrition. The vast majority of the population is rural and there are immense land pressures due to the high population density to begin with, but the returning refugees and displaced persons.

So the numbers of issues that have gone unaddressed by the current government that has been in power for 10 years have led to a very, very unsatisfied, dissident population. Ironically, and I point this out in my written testimony but I won't elaborate here, Nkurunziza has been a popular President with the rural population, overall, and my own private opinion is that he could have easily won this election doing it without any kind of manipulation, and it is a shame that what has occurred, has occurred. That it really didn't need to. The third party issue should have been solved by the constitutional court and been just a legal issue that Burundi solved in and of itself.

But it is important to know that the tensions in the country are real. The Imbonerakure youth gangs that Elavie mentioned are organized and active. They have been around actually since 2012 or maybe even before. They are often uniformed. They carry weapons. They operate mostly at night. They intimidate. They harass. They even kill. People often sleep outside their homes in rural areas for fear that the Imbonerakure youth gangs might show up. Even with the flow of refugees out of the country, Imbonerakure, according to information I am getting particularly in the north part of the country in Kayanza, have been intercepting refugees as they are trying to leave the country to go into Rwanda, taking away their belongings and even raiding in their houses in the evening to take furniture and stuff out of it.

So they are continuing to intimidate population. The government has said of course that it is trying to disarm the Imbonerakure. That effort is moving very slow. Again, an issue that we may not all be aware of is the fact that since the ceasefire in 2003 and 2004, the efforts to get guns out of the population's hands, out of civilian population have been basically a failure. Some estimates estimate that as high as 300,000 weapons still exist out there in the civilian population.

Weapons of choice are grenades. Grenades are plentiful. They are easy to hide, put them in your pocket, throw them into a group of people quite easily. We see that all the time. The most egregious one was in Gatumba in 2011. You remember when 40 people were killed in a bar.

And then we have the refugee flows. I am sure you are aware that recent reporting by MSF says 1,000 people a day are crossing into Rwanda right now. Aljazeera was just reporting yesterday from the camp there, where there is 70,000 refugees now in Rwanda, up to 170,000 total including Tanzania. So these are very, very real situations. There was fighting on July 10 in Kayanza which reportedly was with the armed forces and a group of rebels, who probably are former armed forces or involved in the coup, and they are well armed and they are staging in the Kibira forest area.

So those tensions occur, continue to occur, and will be real for the time being and into the future, so it is a very tense situation that we are faced with. Undoubtedly, in a few days' time or by August 26th, we will, the West will be faced with a Nkurunziza-led government. Not happy with the way he got there possibly, but he will be there. We will have to deal with him. And while many countries are withdrawing their security assistance, other forms of aid including, as you well know, some of the aid that was coming in for the election process itself was withdrawn by three donors.

Short of breaking diplomatic relations and cutting off ties, what is it that we can do to help to bring Burundi to a peaceful, sustained peaceful future? My colleagues have already named a number of things with which I agree. I think it is really important that we remain, first of all, we remain outspoken, which we have been doing. The new Special Envoy is good to have in place. We, along with the United Nations and the African Union, have said the right things recently. We need to push publicly and strongly for upholding democratic principles, the rule of law, freedom of press—extremely important. As we all know the press was shut down. A lot of the press was shut down during the crisis—but also for independent judiciary and independent elections commission.

Part of the problem with the third term issue was the doubt cast upon the constitutional court's validity and so we need to push hard for that independence of the judiciary. We need to revive and strengthen the efforts of local NGOs, and NGOs like the international ones that are working there that are represented at this table. Community groups and religious organizations, we need to restart efforts to promote reconciliation and peace efforts across political, community, subregional, religious, and ethnic lines.

And again I refer to those efforts that led us up to the 2005 elections and through that which did have success. They can be done. We need to push and assist, which we can do, in this disarmament effort. The government says it is working on the disarmament effort. Let us hold it at its word. Let us push for that. Let us offer resources for that if we can.

I think it is important that we mobilize and continue to mobilize greater national attention to the rising political and ethnic threat that Burundi represents to the country and to the region. Congresswoman Bass, here, asked about the region. We know tensions exist in the region. We know the relationships with Rwanda and

Burundi are problematic and have been for some years going back to 1994 and before. We know that some staging of rebel groups, Banyamulenge and others, are rumored to be happening in the DRC. We know the FNL itself, one of the opposition parties has done some staging there.

So we need to work with the regional group countries and to, as I said, push strongly to see that they do nothing to exacerbate the tensions in Burundi. Make it clear to President Nkurunziza and his closest allies and associates that they have violated international agreements and norms in their actions and that they bear the greatest responsibility for the current political crisis. They will be held responsible to the international community for any breakdown in the future in law and order and any mass violence that should occur.

I think in this context that, Alissa mentioned this, that we should push for the establishment of the Truth and Reconciliation Commission, which is of course an Arusha Accords mandated body and has not yet come into effect. A little goes a long way to getting toward questions of justice. There should be no immunity for violent deeds by youth militias like Imbonerakure, the police, or any other party that is engaged in violence and loss of life because this isn't all just one-sided obviously. It is important to realize that this crisis did not catch the world unaware.

Since 2008, when preparations for the 2010 elections began and in subsequent years, international funding for democracy and governance, as Mike as talked about, and reconciliation and peacebuilding has fallen away. The work with political party reconciliation, leadership development and integration and capacity building of the armed forces that was done through those years needs to be continued.

The issue of making sure we have long-term commitments has been mentioned by everybody at this table, and it just seems to be something that never, ever gets through to policymakers. You never get a grant for more than 18 months to 2 years anyway no matter what you are doing, and as soon as you have done it then you have done that and the donor moves on to something else and somebody else. And just when you are beginning to establish yourselves and beginning to be effective and have impact, whether you are local, whether you are international NGOs, that gets withdrawn.

Then another thing that I want to mention, just in closing, which Burundi officials will not like, and that is we often say to ourselves, and you hear this from the U.S. Government officials, that, well, we have such limited leverage, what can we do; how can we push? Well, it is true. We don't want to be in a position of taking away humanitarian aid and assistance and et cetera that is so badly needed. We don't want to break diplomatic relations. We don't want to do those things.

But remember that there is one point of leverage that should be borne in mind. I am not threatening anybody, but in terms of Burundi's role in international peacekeeping in Haiti, Central African Republic, Cote d'Ivoire, Sudan, where it has over 7,200 troops committed, nearly one fifth of the standing armed National Army is committed to peacekeeping. They have a wonderful reputation, laudable contribution to international peace and order. However, Burundi is reimbursed by the U.N. $1,028 for each soldier deployed, or a return of $45 million annually, along with salaries of $750 a month received by each individual soldier, 7,200 soldiers. You can add all that up. The Burundi Government should be warned that mass violence in Burundi and any human rights perpetrated by the security forces domestically could jeopardize their ability to serve in future peacekeeping operations. Thank you.

[The prepared statement of Mr. McDonald follows:]

BURUNDI: HOW SHOULD THE INTERNATIONAL COMMUNITY RESPOND?

Testimony before the House of Representatives Subcommittee on Africa, Global Health, Global Human Rights, and International Organizations

Steve McDonald

July 22, 2015

The elections cycle got underway in Burundi on June 29, when the election for the parliamentary bodies, the Senate and National Assembly, took place. A second round of elections was held on July 21, despite almost three months of protests and almost universal condemnation of the president and ruling party for going forward with the elections under the current circumstances. The present crisis began on April 28, when President Pierre Nkurunziza announced that he would seek a third term. Burundi erupted into a chaotic scene of street protests and violent police response, followed by an attempted military coup, refugee flows into neighboring countries, and gangs of youth roaming communities at night intimidating, threatening and even killing their fellow citizens. At least 90 persons have died, maybe more, and up to 160,000 refugees have left the country, most going to Tanzania and Rwanda. Many independent radio stations have been closed, even transmission towers destroyed, to limit the flow of news to Burundians, who receive almost all their information by radio or word of mouth.

The background to this situation is complicated, to say the least. Burundi, as all Africa watchers know, has a history of intercommunal violence, often revolving around elections, which began in 1972 and has accounted for as many as 450,000 deaths over those four decades and massive numbers of refugees and displaced persons. This violent past seemed to have come to an end after the signing of an internationally brokered peace agreement in Arusha, Tanzania, in 2001, a subsequent ceasefire in 2004, and peaceful elections in 2005 that brought Nkurunziza to power. Nkurunziza, who had been a university professor, led an armed group, the CNDD-FDD,[1] in rebellion against the sitting government for over a decade. The CNDD-FDD had not signed the Arusha Peace Accords, but did agree to the ceasefire in 2004 and transformed itself into a political party.

---

[1] National Council for the Defense of Democracy-Forces for the Defense of Democracy (Conseil national pour la defense de la democratie-Forces pour la defense de la democratie).

Despite the current turmoil, Nkurunziza had proved to be a popular president in the past. He was a master at old time populism, spending inordinate amounts of time in the countryside interacting with people, attending church, playing soccer - his favorite pastime - and joining in planting cassava and other crops with subsistence farmers. A Gallup Poll in 2011 that gauged the popularity of African heads of state listed Nkurunziza as the most popular on the continent, coming in with an 89% approval rating. This, despite the fact that his government had been ineffective, done little to create jobs or enhance revenue flows, and was massively corrupt. Even with irregularities at the polling places, violence, and opposition boycotts, he won reelection in 2010 with 91.62% of the votes cast. Few observers thought he would lose a free and fair election in 2015.

The question that prompted the protests and subsequent violence, however, was not on his popularity but whether or not Nkurunziza had the right to run under the Arusha Accords and subsequent constitutional term limits provisions. Even before he had announced his intention to run there was an outcry from almost every quarter that he should not, including the UN Special Envoy for the Great Lakes, the Secretary General of the UN, the European Community, the Africa Union, the East African Community, and individual governments like the United States. Even a group of "elders" from within the ruling party privately counseled Nkurunziza not to run.

In fact, this issue is a rather fine legal point. The Arusha Accords and the constitution, established after Arusha, both prohibit more than two terms for a president. But, the logic used by Nkurunziza and his supporters was that in 2005 he was not popularly elected. The vote was carried out on a party list basis and the CNDD-FDD got a majority in parliament. By procedures set by the Arusha Accords, the National Assembly then appointed the president. Nkurunziza was that appointee and became president. He had not, however, run for president and, therefore, had the right to run again for two terms via popular direct election.

The legal point is obviously murky and open to interpretation. Opponents state that the intention or "spirit" of the Arusha Accords and subsequent constitution was to limit a president to two terms no matter how he came into office. Nkurunziza supporters counter that the international community and the parliament had plenty of time to make that clarification into law, but did not. Therefore, with both sides having some rationale behind their views, this seems a legality that should have been left for the Constitutional Court to decide on its constitutionality. So it was and the court ruled in favor of Nkurunziza having a third term. That should have been the end of the matter, at least legally, but the court's ruling was discredited when the vice president of the court fled the country and issued a statement that he and fellow justices had been threatened and coerced into the ruling by the government. A number of the "elders" who had advised against a third term, including the Second Vice President and the Speaker of the Assembly, have also fled in the fear of their safety.

The volatility of this issue had been known for years, with a formal "Situational Analysis" prepared in October 2013 for the United Nations Department of Political Affairs at the request of the Secretary General concluding that "should President Nkurunziza get an interpretation of the constitution that he feels justifies a third term, and choose to seek one, the likelihood of violent response increases immensely. An announcement to this effect would be a major flashpoint for violence even in his own party."

It is important to note that the response of street protests was not unique to Burundi. It is akin to what happened earlier in Senegal and Burkina Faso where presidents abrogated constitutional term limits and were met with public protest, and often met that protest with oppressive and deadly force. In each of these cases the president either was defeated at the polls (Senegal), or stepped down after extended public unrest (Burkina Faso). The protests in Burundi reflect the same growing demand found in many African countries for greater democratization and adherence to the rule of law. This represents a changing Africa, which has seen growing public protest since the end of the Cold War for greater adherence to constitutional norms, respect for human rights, and the accountability of their leaders.

It also reflects rising popular dissatisfaction with the continuing condition in which the people of Burundi find themselves. In fact, Burundi is one of the poorest countries on earth with one of the lowest levels of human development in the world, being at the bottom of Heavily Indebted Poor Countries (HIPC) standings, one of 39 countries so designated in 2015 by the International Monetary Fund. Approximately 80% of Burundi's population lives in poverty. Famines and food shortages occur frequently and, according to the World Food Program, 56.8% of children under age five suffer from chronic malnutrition. At $420 per year, Burundi's per capita GDP is second-lowest in the world. Although Burundi's largest economic sector is agriculture (it accounts for 58% of national GDP), subsistence agriculture accounts for 90% of the agriculture base.

Commercial crops only constitute a tenth of agricultural output, predominately with the export of coffee. Low and unreliable electricity supply - less than two percent of Burundians have access to electricity and only 1.2 percent of the population use the internet - contributes to limited prospects for manufacturing and industry, thus stymying economic investment and growth. The Global Competitiveness Index ranks Burundi at or near the bottom of its country rankings for infrastructure, macroeconomic environment, technological readiness, business sophistication, and innovation.

Furthermore, inflation is a serious problem, with food and petrol prices rising and an inflation rate at 7.5% for 2015, down from an average of 14.5% in 2012. Add to this an unemployment rate that might run as high as 40% with no significant manufacturing or industry in this rural economy. Youth unemployment overall is probably near 60%. Land pressures are immense in a country that has one of the highest population densities in the world (396 persons per square kilometer of land as of 2013, the latest figures available) and has been facing the return of refugees and displaced persons from the earlier conflicts.

All of these elements, unemployment, rising prices, and abject poverty are a fact of life for the average Burundian and, combined with a government riven with corruption and inefficiency, and small arms leftover from the disarmament of the warring parties after 2004 still numbering between 100,000-300,000 in the countryside, provide the flashpoints for violence which have been in place for a long time. In fact, since the disputed elections of 2010, violence has been common throughout the country, to include politically motivated youth gangs intimidating opponents, grenades being tossed into public places frequented by adherents of one or the other of the political parties (one of the most egregious was in October 2011 in a bar-restaurant in Gatumba that left as many as 40 persons dead), and growing incidents of sexual violence. In fact, in early March 2015 there was a public strike over high fuel prices, telephone fees and food costs.

So, the outburst of protest in April was more remarkable for its lack of violence in the beginning, rather than the fact that it occurred. Violence became a factor only after police began using live ammunition against protesters. However, the political issue of the third term was a trigger, not the sole cause. Still, the international media too often casts any conflict in Burundi in historical terms as an Interethnic, inter-communal, majority Hutu versus minority Tutsi struggle without looking at the other, core causes, or investigating the changing nature of ethnic relations in the country. In fact, while there are historical roots to the conflict, the one thing it is not, at present, is ethnically driven. While stability has eluded Burundi in recent years, the one positive outcome of the last 15 years since the signing of the Arusha Accords, has been a society that has largely overcome the ethnic divisions which had provided the fault line along which political rivalries of the past were played out.

Even though ethnicity is not the driving force behind these protests, the danger in Burundi for this conflict to take on ethnic dimensions is palpable and growing. Should the protests, termed "insurgency" by the government, keep escalating, the country is in danger of sliding into days of old when conflict in Burundi was divided along ethnic lines. A strong warning to this effect was issued during a recent visit in June by Adama Deng, UN Special Representative for Genocide. Over the radio, hate speech is beginning as elements in government are identifying predominantly Tutsi neighborhoods as the locus of the agitators. Imbonerakure, which are youth gangs from the ruling party, are terrorizing certain rural areas, intimidating opposition, threatening and even killing on occasion and their targets are primarily Hutu. Burundians, Tutsi and Hutu alike, live in fear. In the night, a knock on the door can mean disaster and many people now sleep outside or pretend not to be home to avoid victimization. It is important to note that little international coverage exists outside Bujumbura, and, although the capital city has been relatively calm of late, disturbing reports from individual Burundians in hotspots like Cibitoke, north of the city and Makamba province in the south of the country, show that intimidation and victimization is going on unchecked. But, the nexus of conflict is basically Hutu versus Hutu, with the most prominent challenger to Nkurunziza being Agathon Rwasa, leader of the FNL (National Liberation Forces), which is a Hutu group that had fought the former Tutsi-dominated government and army, as well as the CNDD-FDD, from which it had splintered during the war years.

Along with the possibility of this situation eventually evolving into a conflict along inter-ethnic, intercommunal fault lines as it was from 1972-2004, it also has profound implications for the Great Lakes Region. Already there are tensions among neighboring states Tanzania, Uganda and Rwanda over the different positions that have taken on Nkurunziza's third-term bid and the attempted coup against him. These tensions could deepen if violence mounts and refugee flows continue. The possible staging or harboring of dissident forces opposing Nkurunziza in eastern Democratic Republic of the Congo (DRC) could reignite open conflict there and further damage inter-state relations. Rumors are already rife that elements of the Banyamulenge in North and South Kivu in the DRC coming to support protesters against Nkurunziza. Fighting on July 10 in Kayanza province in northeast was reportedly between the army and dissident former army members who had supported the coup, were staging in the Kibera Forest, and were heavily armed.

With no sign of relenting on Nkurunziza's part, the international community is left standing on the sidelines now as the election process plays itself out. The parliamentary elections have finished, despite the opposition boycott and targeted violence during and after the polls. The CENI (the Independent National Elections Commission) issued a statement on July 2 that the vote was free, and had proceeded in a calm and peaceful manner with "no incidents reported" despite intimidation in certain quartiers. The turnout, it said, was "massive" with 95% of registered voters casting ballots. The CNDD-FDD reportedly won 77 seats, government allied parties won 2 seats, and the boycotting opposition won 21 seats. However, because of constitution mandates on ethnic and gender percentages, the government held a conference on July 9 to determine who would take those seats and meet the percentage requirements, appointing some opposition candidates and replacing others with their own members. It is fair to say the CNDD-FDD now has almost complete control of parliament.

At present, Uganda President Yoweri Museveni has led a delegation to Burundi to try and launch an inter-party dialogue. As of July 17, the delegation, now led by the Defense Minister Crispus Kiyonga with Museveni's departure, has begun a dialogue to which opposition leaders like Agathon Rwasa and Charles Nditije have committed. Kiyonga has said he is committed to continue this effort until the parties have reached an accommodation on the future.

Presidential elections take place on July 22 and every indication is Nkurunziza will win those. He will have no opposition and continued intimidation in opposition areas will keep votes for other candidates from being cast. So, all international players will be faced with a probable post-election scenario similar to Kenya after the 2007 elections or Cameroon more recently, where violence occurred, elections irregularities were rife, and a president now sits in office despite an unsavory process and actions on his part. Will the world just accept it as business as usual, as was done with Cameroon, where, because of economic and security ties, the West has ignored a president who has been in power through rigged elections for 31 years and runs one of the most corrupt governments in Africa? What avenues will be open to the Western governments and international institutions in response? Can they, with good conscience, stop developmental and humanitarian aid to the people to punish Nkurunziza? Will they push for sanctions a la Zimbabwe? Or, will they say business as usual? The world doesn't want to do the former and does not have to do the latter. Here are a set of responses that the international community should consider, even while maintaining diplomatic relations and keeping humanitarian aid flowing.

1. Push publicly and strongly for upholding democratic principles, the rule of law, freedom of the press, an independent judiciary and an independent election commission.

2. Revive and strengthen efforts by local NGOs, community groups and religious organizations to prevent mass violence associated with elections opponents and ethnic conflict that may emerge from the current crisis. Re-start efforts to promote reconciliation and peace efforts across political, community, sub-regional, religious and ethnic lines, efforts that proved very effective in the lead-up to the 2005 elections.

3. Mobilize greater international attention to the rising political and ethnic threat that Burundi represents to the country and the region. While still a remote possibility, the international community should monitor events with an eye to genocide prevention.

4. Strongly encourage regional states to not engage in activities that will further destabilize Burundi or provoke greater political or ethnic conflict there or in the region more broadly.

5. Make it clear that President Nkurunziza and his closet political associates that they have violated international agreements and norms in their actions and that they bear the greatest responsibility for the current political crisis. They will be held responsible by the international community for any breakdown in any law and order or any mass violence that has occurred as a result of their political actions.

6. There should be no immunity from violent deeds by youth militias like Imbonerakure, the police, or any other party that has engaged in violence and loss of life. Establishing a Truth and Reconciliation Commission should be urged as a priority.

7. It is important to realize that this crisis did not catch the world unaware. Since 2008, when preparations began for the 2010 elections and in subsequent years as they were underway for 2015, international funding for democracy and governance (D&G) support, reconciliation and peace building has fallen away dramatically. The US embassy had no D&G funds in its budget for the years 2010 -2014. The work with political party reconciliation, leadership development and the integration and capacity building of the armed forces command that had occurred between 2002-2008, was discontinued. We cannot ignore the preparation and lead-up to the next elections cycle in 2020 as we have done for the last two.

8. Burundi's role in international peacekeeping in Somalia, the Central African Republic, Cote d'Ivoire, Sudan and Haiti, where it has over 7,200 troops committed, nearly one fifth of their standing National Army –has been a laudable contribution to international peace and order. However, Burundi is reimbursed by the UN $1,028 for each soldier deployed, or a return of $45 million annually, along with the salaries of $750 a month received directly by the soldiers. The Burundian government should be warned that mass violence in Burundi and any human rights perpetrated by their security forces domestically could jeopardize their ability to serve in future peacekeeping operations.

Mr. SMITH. Thank you very much, Mr. McDonald. Let me say for the record, Tom Perriello as well as Secretary Linda Thomas Greenfield were invited. They had things that they are doing overseas. We have invited them at a date when they can make themselves available. I think that will happen. So part two of this hearing will be to hear from them, and probably more from the NGO side as well, sometime in September.

We also submit for the record and unanimous consent, a statement by Assistant Professor Cara Jones and a letter from the Ambassador of Burundi to the United States. Without objection, so ordered.

I thought since we have a series of votes coming, I, my good colleague Ms. Bass, and Mr. Donovan will ask questions and then we will see if we have time for a second round, if there are anything you didn't answer or we want to elaborate, we will do it that way.

Let me begin the questioning, first, with July 2, 2015, just a few weeks ago, days ago, the State Department announced that they were going to suspend security assistance programs to Burundi. What do you think needs to be done to resume that money? As specific as possible would be appreciated. What role have neighboring states played in either fomenting or addressing Burundi's crisis? Is Kagame playing a role here? We have heard that. I would appreciate your thoughts on that.

Mr. Jobbins, you went into great detail and appropriate detail about the impact in your part, backdrop of desperation that USAID funded research in 2010, 45 percent of the children under 5 are anemic, and NGO's report stunting rates of 57 percent. As you know, Burundi signed up to the scaling up program in February 2013, which is this herculean effort on the first thousand days of life from conception to the second birthday. If you get that right, the next 25,000–30,000 days of that child's life into adulthood will be exponentially enhanced in terms of immunity, strength, stunting pretty much goes away, but that prenatal care, mother and baby of course, maternal healthcare is absolutely transformational. They signed up in 2013; how well or poorly are they doing, if you can speak to that.

Let me also ask about, Ms. Wilson, you emphasized the importance of the faith community. Maybe all of you might want to elaborate how they are being on all sides, all faith community leaders into the peace efforts, the mitigation of ethnic animosities. Is that working? Do they utilize the faith community as effectively as they could?

Ms. Wilson, you talked about how revitalizing the mediation process should be the top priority for the United States. Is it? Are we doing it? If not, are we about to do it? And I do have other questions. And the 150-plus journalists, did any of them encounter any threats, pushback? Were they unfettered in their ability to report on and to ascertain what is truly going on?

Ms. BASS. Sure, I just have a couple of questions really focusing on the U.S. and what more we can do, in particular with the IDPs and the concern about people being in the surrounding countries and what more that we can do on the human rights side, on the humanitarian side, but also on the security side.

And then the AU has taken a position that they will not recognize the results of the election which, although they haven't been announced, everybody knows what the results are going to be, and so I wanted to get a sense as to practically what that means. Will the President not be allowed to participate in the AU? Will he be kicked out? How do you see that in whether or not you see that is going to have any impact on him? Those are my two questions.

Mr. DONOVAN. I, as is the chairman, very concerned about the children. And I met with a group yesterday, we were talking about preventable diseases that we have medicines and inoculations for, and also about the malnutrition that you spoke about, Mike, and wondering if the aid being provided, first of all, is it being provided for the children?

Doctor, I have a 2-month old and I am so glad to hear you say about the children, how they are cherished in your country.

So, one, is aid being provided? Is medication being provided for these preventable diseases, and is food being provided to help with this malnutrition? And two, if it is being provided, is it getting to the children or is the government allowing the aid to be received by those who are in need? So those are my two issues.

Mr. JOBBINS. Thank you so much. To take first perhaps the cross-cutting question of nutrition and food security. We have seen some progress with a lot of different assistance programs to ensure food security, but what we haven't seen is that the fundamental underlying mathematics is broken of this agricultural society that doesn't have enough land with the agricultural techniques to feed its people. And so the question for the long term is not how do we ensure food security right now, but how do we set a path for growth? And that is only through regional integration, it is only through an education system that prepares people for the modern economy and through dealing with this urban class. And so I think to us that is the biggest gap. Certainly emergency feeding is needed, but setting people up for a path for growth is what we haven't seen a lot of progress on and what is absolutely critical.

But to come to terms with Mr. Smith's question about the media, we did feel that with the journalists who we worked with—we worked with six radio stations as well as our own journalists—we were able to document what happened on voting day. However, this is a current against the backdrop of, like Steve said, a number of radio stations are off-air. We have in principle the President as well as certainly the media themselves want to get back on air, but there is a lot of very deep issues about the pre-conditions for those to get back on air.

And in terms of where, places where there could be found common ground, certainly every political actor in Burundi has been the victim of hate speech at one point or another in their careers and everyone has benefited from the opportunity to have a fair shake through the media. And so to the extent that that can be an opportunity to get those stations back on air to meet the concerns of the government, get them back on air can help create the conditions for a dialogue to be successful. It is a key confidence building measure and one where we feel that there is a decent chance at least of beginning to set things on the right course in supporting that dialogue and social compact.

To touch just rapidly on the two questions of the faith communities and the displaced. The faith communities have played a heroic role particularly on the aspect of preventing violence. We have worked with interfaith groups throughout this crisis. I was meeting with them the day before protests broke out about how you talk about violence to your parishioners or to your congregations. And the number one message that they focused on was the principle of individual accountability, the story of Cain and Abel in the Christian tradition.

At the end of the day, you alone are accountable for your acts before the law and before God. It is not your commander. It is not your neighbor. It is not your political leader who is going to be rendering an account for the judgment, but in fact it is going to be you yourself who have to justify your own actions. That has been something that has been particularly empowering and something that needs to be reinforced. That principle does not group collective blame but rather every individual has the right and the responsibility to for their own actions, and the faith community has been very instrumental in communicating that as a moral message.

And then the last question on the displaced people, we see that there has been a slow increase in assistance. Right now the capacity is still overwhelmed particularly in Tanzania and Rwanda with the reports of the latest, there seems to be signs it is being overwhelmed. And in Congo, of course refugees are fleeing into an area that is profoundly unstable and risks destabilizing further the context of the Ruzizi Plains on the Congolese side.

But what we hear from our colleagues—we work in each of those countries. What we hear from our colleagues are two other needs in addition to the humanitarian needs. One is access to information, media programming and information that can help prevent those populations from being manipulated. We have seen in past crises in the region how refugees have been instrumentalized, have been manipulated into worsening the violence back home, and that is something that will absolutely be critical.

And then the second is the issue of protection. We hear particularly our colleagues, from talking with the Tanzanian Government, there are a lot of concerns in how the government themselves can ensure protection for these vulnerable populations, for victims, for women, for children who are fleeing, how you ensure their security, how you ensure their wellbeing in this crisis. It is something that in those areas the government hasn't had a lot of experience and capacity and resources for.

And so to the extent that we can focus on the protection of women, children, victims of violence in those refugee settings is a key point that has been underlined to us by the humanitarian community and by the governments of those neighboring countries. I think I will let my colleagues speak to those points, and then also about the regional actors.

Ms. NDURA. Let me focus on children's issues. I can say that I am a grandma. I always start with the children and I end with the children. It is almost like when you travel across Burundi, it is very much as if it's two worlds ''juxtaposed'' to each other. Even within the same provinces, you go to an area in the city centers or a neighborhood where children are very well cared for, have everything they need, even more than they need. They are spoiled to death even, sometimes, and have a great education. They are multilingual, sometimes in French and Swahili because they have the best schools. And then you walk a mile or two to just see children who are in the dirt, many times with not even the basic clothing on, honestly, naked in the street in the water puddles after it rains. And then of course with all the germs or the illnesses that that brings to them.

So when I travel and work across Burundi I always ask myself that same question, where is all the assistance that all these multinations are saying they have poured into Burundi? I personally have not seen it. I am being honest. I really have not seen it. Because I was able to travel to Burundi for the first time in 2006, because I was a political refugee I had to wait for my U.S. passport for which I will forever be grateful. That is what allowed me to go back to Burundi to do the work that I currently do.

But you don't see, I have not been seeing. In 2006, I thought this is normal. The country is barely emerging from armed conflict so it is normal that everybody is hungry, that everybody is poor. But how about today, 2015? I was there in March. The conditions have not changed. So I don't see where the support is going. So what do we do? Do we stop? Definitely not. Because if we were to stop the assistance, then many more children, many more expectant mothers would die.

I would say expect accountability. How do we do that? Burundi, it is very difficult to operate and to collaborate with people from different cultures, because if we ask for reports about how the assistance has been spent and we get the reports but that is not always how exactly how things were done, and we proclaim that things were done because we have a report. The report is not always the reality.

So I suggest that not only we continue the assistance to the children and to the mothers, but actually increase it. But also monitor, more effective monitoring practices from people who have a greater conscience. I don't want us to do like one country in Europe did. They gave cows to a community, three cows, and then they sent three consultants, one per cow. And one consultant per cow and they were paid $15,000 to watch over the cow. No, that is not what I am proposing.

But we surely need a more effective monitoring process that would ensure that the assistance gets there, that it is distributed, so that we can increase it. There are very responsible people in Burundi, we just need to find them. There are people who are compassionate in Burundi, we just need to find them. Because most of the time those that we reach immediately because they have access to us, they have access to these important people with whom they have been working for years, sometimes you may be surprised that they may not be the best.

Moment of truth here. Seriously, I did research on NGOs, community based peacebuilding programs and practices a few years back, and one of the lessons I learned was that oh, how come all the NGO heads and Presidents, how come they are all Tutsis? I noticed, but they still talked to me and I appreciated the work they did. But as a researcher I still have to ask myself. So who has access to us and whom do we have access to has to be reconceptualized to make sure our good work really produces the impact that it is meant to have.

Now beyond children there is youth. Children are not the same as youth. Let me go back to the youth. Until we invest in sustained opportunities to provide the youth with the means to produce their own food, their own money to take care of themselves, to go to the clinic when they are sick, to take care of their wives and children when they get married and have families, until we show them that they do not need to depend on biased and self-serving political party leaders—there must be a category for enhancing and developing the capacity of youth to productively engage in the affairs of Burundi—I am sitting here to say the troubles of Burundi will continue. Because when those young men, young women are hungry, they will do whatever they need to get food. We are just talking about food. We are not talking about cars and houses and boats. We are talking about basic needs, food, medicine, shelter. The youth. There must be a category—yes, the children. We need to help them grow in a safe neighborhood. But there must be a new emphasized category for the youth. Until we listen, we are not helping Burundi and the Burundian people.

Ms. WILSON. Two quick points. First, on the mediation. So as you mentioned before, we had not had as robust a presence as we might have in this process because we didn't have a Special Envoy appointed. And so I would say right now we have a hopeful moment that someone is there and can really be the U.S. point person on collaborating with these partners. But I would say that two mediators were dismissed from this process and now we are on to a new process.

And I would say that it has been harder to see how and whether the Burundian NGOs that we mentioned, that Steve has mentioned, will be consulted and what that consultation will look like. And if it happens in a black box, to come back to the Burundian people and explain what has happened will be harder than if there was a process that did involve these kinds of organizations.

Also on the role of faith, someone said to me that people are believers before they are political beings, and I thought that was just a really salient point. Because there is a reach that faith communities have that others don't have just because of the moral authority often that faith leaders play. And it is not always easy, and it is not always that faith leaders are apolitical beings, but that there is a higher sense that they are trying to work toward.

And as Search for Common Ground as done, as we have done, I think, in supporting the faith leaders who really want to come together and ensure that both at the local level and at the national level, these messages for dialogue are really being heard in the community. And as I mentioned, it is happening across the country, and I think as long as that continues we have a hope line for what can happen both within civil society and at the sociopolitical level.

Ms. NDURA. And may I add that even with the faith community we cannot go in without thinking and asking critical questions? One of the things I noticed when I traveled to Burundi is that many of the guests at hotels, sometimes large numbers, are always missionaries, mostly from the United States. So there are financial advantages for many Burundians for connecting with those missionaries because they bring dollars.

So are we practicing faith because we are called by the Almighty to improve the wellbeing of the Burundian people or are we preaching and praising the Almighty because He, or She—who knows? I haven't seen Him. I believe, but I don't know. Are we praising the Almighty because He has helped us connect with somebody who would help us complete the foundation for our new home?

Do you know that President Nkurunziza is one of the most practicing faithful people? He prays a lot. He even dances for the Lord. Is he listening more? Should he listen more? Is he growing from his faith that tells him to love all people and care for people, to actually develop and exact policies that will help him and his associates live by faith? I would just end with that question.

Mr. McDonald. I want to respond to several of the questions, but I will start where Elavie and Alissa ended, first of all, just by saying quite simply that I have not been to a country in Africa—and I have been to almost every sub-Saharan African country for an extended period of time in my life—that is more faith-based, is more religious than Burundi. It is a deeply, deeply religious people. But I absolutely agree with what Elavie said. President Nkurunziza has been here for the Presidential Prayer Breakfast. He has been wined and dined by all kinds of faith-based people and organizations, and we have got to be very careful how we approach this issue. That is all I will say on that.

Mediation process, not a whole lot more to say than what Alissa said. I think it has not been a top priority, which was your question, Congressman Smith, but it should be and hopefully is being underlined even more now. I am aware of a process that is going on right now in The Hague where the Burundi Leadership Training Program, an organization that I had a lot to do with coming into being, and The Netherlands Institute for Multiparty Democracy are meeting with State Department officials from the Bureau of Conflict Stabilization Operations talking about exactly this effort. We need to encourage, we need to enlarge on that. It is an area in which we can have an effect.

But also to your question on the regional role, regional states' role, Uganda of course was doing, I think, a very honest mediation role in the past few days, so let us not ignore the neighboring states as potential players in the mediation process. As far as what we should be saying to neighboring states, I think it goes back to that old platitude, first of all do no harm, because that is possible.

I am not an expert in this area, but there are certainly rumors about that Rwanda has possibly tried to instigate anti-Tutsi fears, and whether this is happening officially or not we don't know. But certainly tensions are building, and as I said in my oral remarks, the tensions in the eastern DRC organizations and groups that are there, FDLR, Banyamulenge, et cetera, have got to be very careful that they don't get involved in this. So we really need to be consulting with all the neighboring states at all times.

In this security sector assistance, I think the United States has done exactly the right thing in terms of stopping that assistance right now. I think we have got a situation in some ways, and analogous to Nigeria now, we want to be helpful in Nigeria in the fight against Boko Haram, but how can you work with a military that is corrupt and ineffective and inefficient? So you have got to be sure you have some security sector reform before you can move back in there. It is not very easy.

The army, as Mike said, has been one of the positive things in this whole crisis and transition and that is good, but they are not without their own divisions particularly from the intelligence unit which is very close to President Nkurunziza. But they are very well meaning, professional army officers of both Tutsi and Hutu backgrounds with whom we can work. What we can do is have a very, very effective well plugged-in defense attache there who is following these things very, very closely.

And I am not quite sure what the status of that is with our Embassy. I am a very, very big supporter of Ambassador Liberi. I think she is doing a wonderful job, but I think she is limited in her staff and her outreach and her ability to get at some of these issues. So that maybe needs to be one thing we build up just to know more about those divisions within the army, and when the time will come when we can work with them again in terms of security sector assistance.

In some ways that is the same thing I can say about the refugee issues. Mike has elaborated on that a bit. One thing is we need to be better informed. I don't think anybody from our Embassy in Tanzania has been to the border yet to visit with those refugee camps. I know they haven't gone yet to the Rwanda border because those camps have just popped up there, literally just popped up there overnight. Obviously we have got to work very closely with the U.N. High Commissioner for Refugees on that, but our own efforts to inform ourselves need to be increased.

The other thing was your question, Congresswoman Bass, on not recognizing this election and what happens next. I am reminded, I can pull my gray beard out on this and I am reminded of what happened after the Idi Amin coup in Uganda, and I was in Uganda at that time as a political officer in the American Embassy. And the OAU had a really tough time knowing who to seat at the 10th anniversary of the OAU up in Addis Ababa when Idi Amin and Milton Obote both showed up. It can be a difficult issue.

But the AU is not the OAU. They operate by some pretty different rules and it is a much better organization. But still, I think the fact of the matter will be, as I said in my testimony we will be faced with a government that we will have to recognize. That it will be a de facto situation that we will have to deal with. How the AU handles that, how we handle it diplomatically I will leave to other people to sort out. But it is going to be a fait accompli. And in time, there may be some awkward moments over the next few months, but in time they will be accepted and we will have to work with him and with the Nkurunziza government one way or another. I think that is all.

Mr. SMITH. We still have a few minutes before the votes, so just a couple of follow-up questions. Mr. McDonald, in your testimony you talked about a novel idea which would cost Burundi some $45 million if they were disqualified from participating in peacekeeping. They have the deployments in Somalia, Cote d'Ivoire,

Sudan, Haiti, Central African Republic, and the numbers are rather stark, $45 million and $750 per month for the soldiers as you point out, one-fifth of the standing army. And I do believe, and correct me if I am wrong, that that actually helps make them a better, not worse, military force because of the humanitarian work they do.

But I remember when Mr. Jobbins testified on the Central African Republic almost 2 years ago, pointed out to our committee that the Burundi deployments were among the most professional, if not the most professional that you saw, which is a paradox. Is it the police that is really the problem, or the military? If you two might want to elaborate on that. Because I think I know what you are trying to get at, Mr. McDonald, and it is a laudable goal to try to have some impact on the government. But again I think those peacekeeping operations might be harmed. I am not sure enough could be raised up in any reasonable amount of time, but again they are among the most professional, which is a paradox.

Secondly, on the issue of the first thousand days from conception to the second birthday, the numbers are not really coming down. And I am not sure with the big sign-up ceremony in February 2013. In other places we have seen it—I was in Guatemala the day the Guatemalan Government signed on to the first thousand days program; with nutrition supplementation for mother and baby, both unborn and newborn, the stunting does come down. In Nigeria, ½ million kids died before the age of 2.

Preventable deaths like few places in the world, and we are hoping—I raised it with President Buhari yesterday that this should be a singular issue that he says, for the sake of the children and the mothers, do you want to mitigate maternal death and morbidity, make sure that there is enough proper nutrition and supplementation for both mother and baby. And again stunting does go away if this were to happen. So if you could maybe elaborate a little bit on that issue, because I think that is a cost-effective initiative that has got a lot of rhetorical support but not a whole lot of implementation on the ground.

And on faith leaders, my real focus is on the pastors, the bishops, the archbishops, the people who I have found, and I have been here 35 years and I remember in Central America it was the church that played pivotal roles. Cardinal Obando y Bravo in Nicaragua, I remember meeting with him when he was under siege, frankly, but they tried to make peace. They tried for human rights to speak truth to power.

And all over Africa, everywhere I go I meet with the faith community, whether Muslim, Orthodox Christian, Roman Catholic, Evangelical and others, Friends, and everywhere I go I find they have that higher calling, as was mentioned, and they put their lives on the line like few people that I know. Now there could be politicians who brandish and wear their faith on their sleeve, but I find that the clergy, they are in it for the people and that is the way they serve God.

And I am just wondering if the U.S. Department of State and USAID, because I have this argument with them all the time, sufficiently understands the asset that they pose? We have been pushing this in South Sudan to get the church more involved. They are ready and willing. I have met with bishops, my staff, Greg and Piero have, and they get put over to the side a little bit. Have a prayer service at the beginning, but they are not really integral parts of this whole process. So if you could speak to that one as well.

Mr. JOBBINS. Thank you so much. I think to the first question about the role that the Burundian troops have played, for example, in the Central African Republic, I said, as you alluded to, several years ago, and it is still is the case that they are playing a very positive role and are certainly cooperating and contributing to protection in that country and in, as far as I understand, a number of the other countries where they are deployed.

I think what I would take away is that you get what you pay for, and security sector reform and a focus on the army reform was an organizing priority and we have seen relatively good performance from the army. There was less of a focus on police reform and less of a focus on justice sector and less of a focus on a number of other elements of the security sector. They have been the groups that have been the most criticized, partially because they haven't been supported through this process.

Second, on the question of nutrition, one of the real achievements of the Nkurunziza's administration and the Government of Burundi with its partners has been child survival. It has been the healthcare extension. It has been also a schooling extension to the rural population that is a source of the popularity of the current government, or one of the reasons that Steve alluded to. There is a lot more that needs to be done fundamentally. For me the challenge is looking at the optimistic scenario, if we are facing 40 percent malnutrition in 2050, it is not how you get from 40 percent to 35 percent, but how do you create the environment for an overall step change in the economy? Fundamentally we do need to work on child survival and agricultural livelihoods, but also how can you set a path for growth so you can get from 40 percent to zero percent? And that is going to be the big political challenge.

Mr. SMITH. On that issue, now I understand immunizations, oral rehydration nutrition therapy, all the pillars of child survival, but are they also doing the first thousand days of life effectively? They signed on, it is just are they doing it? Do you know?

Mr. JOBBINS. For that I am not sure. I don't know the details of all the programs. There are certainly programs underway, but the details I don't know.

And I think the last is just on the question of the religious community. We are supported to an extent for our work with the religious community from the Department of State via the CSO Bureau. Certainly there is always a need for more and more support and particularly in other kinds of domains, but on this immediate question of how can the religious community work with their flocks and their followings to reinforce that message of nonviolence, that component at least is being supported at least to an extent by the Department of State.

But in terms of the broader engagement and the engagement of the religious community as thought partners, I think Museveni's meeting with the religious community as part of his mediation process was a positive one. And certainly as we look to see how that broader social compact could be reinforced beyond the political question of who gets to lead Burundi, but how can we try out a Burundi that people want, certainly the Burundi faith community as well as the media as well as youth groups and community leaders have to play a huge role in that. And so hopefully we will see their political involvement going forward as part of the solution.

Ms. NDURA. The Catholic Church has been one of the most vocal and actively engaged faith groups in Burundi from the beginning. In fact, Le Conseil des eveques, the Bishop's Council was instrumental in leading Burundi to the Arusha Accords in the 2,000 years and before that and they have been very vocal. The only complication is that they have been very vocal against President Nkurunziza's bid for the third term.

So now what I wonder is how would collaboration return, because they do need each other. They need to work together. Burundi is almost 60 percent or so Roman Catholic approximately, a legacy of Belgium, so collaboration is a must between the government and the Roman Catholic Church. I am not clear yet how they will be able to renegotiate that.

But on a smaller scale, my colleague here keeps saying we need to invest more, we need to invest more. George Mason University has had initiatives working to build the youth capacity for peaceful engagement, and we have been doing the work and the collaboration with the Archdiocese, Gitega Archdiocese Office of Education Supervision. And they keep saying we have more ideas, we need to do more work, we need to do more work. But we have yet to generate any kind of financial support that would help us to strengthen and expand the work that they have been doing.

University of Ngozi, also in Burundi, which is interethnic, multifaith, and international, a private institution run by a Catholic priest, is also one of George Mason University's partners. And through our work and collaboration in March, particularly this past March, they were able to organize a youth interfaith festival, therefore enhancing the consciousness of members of different faiths within the university community and beyond to work individually and collectively to promote nonviolence and peace in Burundi. So the faith communities are engaged, but as Mike keeps saying and reminding us, we cannot do the work we need to do without adequate financial support. Our energy can only go so far.

Mr. SMITH. Before you answer, Ms. Wilson, because you might want to incorporate this, on Monday, the Department of State will announce their TIP ratings for human trafficking. And for the record, I wrote that law. It is called the Trafficking Victims Protection Act of 2000. I wrote 2003's and 2005's expansions and reauthorization.

Burundi has a Tier 2 Watch List ranking. And their recommendations—I don't know what it will be Monday, but it might drop to Tier 3, which means a country is an egregious violator. Finalizing a draft legislation on trafficking is one of the recommendations that was made. There were a number of recommendations made by State. What is your sense about the trafficking situation in Burundi today? Because again, Tier 2 Watch List, child sex trafficking, forced labor on plantations, it is a huge problem and I am wondering if the government is doing enough on that, as you go and answer the other questions as well.

Ms. WILSON. I cannot answer that question, but it is something that I will ask some of our colleagues about. And just a small footnote to say that I mentioned time to start planning now for the long-term engagement, because it is hard when you are in the middle of a crisis to think about what is going to happen at the end of a crisis, just as the faith community, as it is consulted by Museveni and others, should be consulted as the U.S. plans for that future part with State, with USAID and others.

Mr. MCDONALD. On the faith leaders issue let me add just one little thing. And that is, in the work that Howard Wolpe and I were involved in and those years that we were involved with a cross section of leadership, we were sure to include the Archbishop of Burundi, several of the provincial archbishops, and Pentecostal and Protestant leaders as well. It is important not just to support the faith-based community and what they do with their flocks, but to be sure they are part of the national dialogue as you begin to build any kind of mediation effort or whatever.

Mr. SMITH. Is State doing that now?

Mr. MCDONALD. Not that I know of.

Ms. NDURA. And sex trafficking, human trafficking, I have not presently collected any data on that but I have witnessed, as I travel a lot in Burundi, it all goes down to poverty. Poverty. People will do whatever they have to do to find food and to find shelter. I guess you realize we have the same problems here in the United States. In the most poor communities that is where we have the greatest problems, relevant problems. That is why I keep going back to the need to intentionally invest in the youth in order to impact any of these problems positively.

Mr. JOBBINS. And I think just to complement on the TIP issue— and thank you so much for your leadership on that and putting protection of vulnerable groups at the forefront of U.S. engagement—we, certainly on the regional sex trafficking, we have certainly heard reports, the extent, I don't think, is documented.

And I think one of the biggest questions both in terms of assistance to the Burundian side, as well as for international groups is understanding the extent to which these very real phenomena are there, but what I can say is that it is almost certain to increase. With one of the highest rates of urbanization in the world you have young, poor migrants moving into cities and to vulnerable situations and increases in street children and other kinds of people living at the margins of society, and so it is very foreseeable that child exploitation, the sexual exploitation of these vulnerable groups is going to increase both in the urban areas as well as many of the reports that we also hear about the artisanal mining communities, where it is not a huge trade in the region but there are artisanal mining activities, and we hear worrying reports about child protection and vulnerable group protection there. So it is certainly a very, very real risk and it is something that needs to be focused on as we focus on these broader issues, how do we really protect that vulnerable group?

Mr. SMITH. Mr. McDonald.

Mr. McDONALD. Well, I will leave the trafficking, because I don't have any statistical evidential thing to put forward on that except in just all of my years of being involved I have seen the trends that are being spoken about by Mike and Elavie, and including in young women and prostitution, Burundians both in DRC and other neighboring countries, so they get there somehow.

On the peacekeeping question that you asked, let me add something there. There is a difference between the police and the military, the army, in terms of how they have responded and how they see their national mission, in my mind. In the work that Wolpe and I did with the military and the integration of the military armed forces, which lasted over a period of about 2½ years with repeated workshops and ongoing efforts at creating a sense of interdependence and trust building, et cetera, none of that was ever done with the police.

Police certainly got technical training from the Belgians and the French and others, but the police of course were transitioning from a gendarmerie to national police situation, old Belgium style, French style gendarmerie, in which sort of the role of them in terms of servants of the people and et cetera just is not quite understood. I think their sense of mission is very different than what the professional army has developed over these years, and that is why the army has performed so very well in its peacekeeping missions abroad.

Now the individual soldiers who have been involved in those peacekeeping missions have been rotated. We are not talking about 7,200 troops stationed over there permanently. So this permeates the army and they are very proud of the professionalism and the reputation they have gained and et cetera, so this is really something to build on. Although the numbers that are abroad at any given time are one-fifth of the armed forces, the entirety of the armed forces have been involved in one way or another in this whole peacekeeping process. And so it really is a point of national pride for them and we should keep that in mind.

Mr. SMITH. Thank you very, very much for your testimonies, your expert guidance. Anything you think we have missed that you would like to add to the record and give us guidance on would be deeply appreciated. But thank you for your time, your expertise, your commitment. It really does make all the difference in the world. The hearing is adjourned.

[Whereupon, at 1:39 p.m., the subcommittee was adjourned.]

APPENDIX

MATERIAL SUBMITTED FOR THE RECORD

SUBCOMMITTEE HEARING NOTICE
COMMITTEE ON FOREIGN AFFAIRS
U.S. HOUSE OF REPRESENTATIVES
WASHINGTON, DC 20515-6128

Subcommittee on Africa, Global Health, Global Human Rights, and International Organizations
Christopher H. Smith (R-NJ), Chairman

July 22, 2015

TO: MEMBERS OF THE COMMITTEE ON FOREIGN AFFAIRS

You are respectfully requested to attend an OPEN hearing of the Committee on Foreign Affairs, to be held by the Subcommittee on Africa, Global Health, Global Human Rights, and International Organizations in Room 2200 of the Rayburn House Office Building (and available live on the Committee website at http://www.ForeignAffairs.house.gov):

DATE: Wednesday, July 22, 2015

TIME: 12:00 p.m.

SUBJECT: The Unfolding Crisis in Burundi

WITNESSES: Mr. Michael Jobbins
                   Director of Global Affairs
                   Search for Common Ground

                   Elavie Ndura, Ph.D.
                   Professor of Education
                   George Mason University

                   Ms. Alissa Wilson
                   Public Education and Advocacy Coordinator for Africa
                   American Friends Service Committee

                   Mr. Steve McDonald
                   Global Fellow
                   Woodrow Wilson International Center for Scholars

By Direction of the Chairman

The Committee on Foreign Affairs seeks to make its facilities accessible to persons with disabilities. If you are in need of special accommodations, please call 202/225-5021 at least four business days in advance of the event, whenever practicable. Questions with regard to special accommodations in general (including availability of Committee materials in alternative formats and assistive listening devices) may be directed to the Committee.

COMMITTEE ON FOREIGN AFFAIRS

MINUTES OF SUBCOMMITTEE ON _Africa, Global Health, Global Human Rights, and International Organizations_ HEARING

Day _Wednesday_ Date _July 22, 2015_ Room _2200 Rayburn HOB_

Starting Time _12:02 p.m._ Ending Time _1:39 p.m._

Recesses | _0_ | (___to___) (___to___) (___to___) (___to___) (___to___) (___to___)

Presiding Member(s)

Rep. Chris Smith

Check all of the following that apply:

Open Session ☑ Electronically Recorded (taped) ☑
Executive (closed) Session ☐ Stenographic Record ☑
Televised ☑

TITLE OF HEARING:

The Unfolding Crisis in Burundi

SUBCOMMITTEE MEMBERS PRESENT:

Rep. Daniel Donovan, Rep. Karen Bass

NON-SUBCOMMITTEE MEMBERS PRESENT: _(Mark with an * if they are not members of full committee.)_

HEARING WITNESSES: Same as meeting notice attached? Yes ☑ No ☐
(If "no", please list below and include title, agency, department, or organization.)

STATEMENTS FOR THE RECORD: _(List any statements submitted for the record.)_

Letter from Ambassador Ernest Ndabashinze, submitted for the record by Rep. Chris Smith
Statement of the Dr. Cara Jones, submitted for the record by Rep. Chris Smith

TIME SCHEDULED TO RECONVENE _____
or
TIME ADJOURNED _1:39 p.m._

Gregory B. Simpkins
Subcommittee Staff Director

MATERIAL SUBMITTED FOR THE RECORD BY THE HONORABLE CHRISTOPHER H. SMITH, A REPRESENTATIVE IN CONGRESS FROM THE STATE OF NEW JERSEY, AND CHAIRMAN, SUBCOMMITTEE ON AFRICA, GLOBAL HEALTH, GLOBAL HUMAN RIGHTS, AND INTERNATIONAL ORGANIZATIONS

EMBASSY OF THE REPUBLIC OF BURUNDI   Washington, D.C., July 21st, 2015

Washington, D.C.

N°204.02/16/.309..../RE/2014

The Honorable Christopher H. Smith
Chairman
Subcommittee on Africa, Global Health,
Global Human Rights and International Organizations
Committee on Foreign Affairs
U.S. House of Representatives
Washington, D.C., 20515

Dear Chairman Smith,

Permit me to express my appreciation for the attention you and your colleagues are paying to my country, **Burundi**, with a special hearing devoted to events there. Burundi and the United States are friends and allies and we take seriously concerns expressed by Members of Congress about the welfare of the Burundian people and wishes for continued success in good governance and constitutional democracy.

As Assistant Secretary of State Linda Thomas-Greenfield said in an interview on the Voice of America on July 15th, "**Burundi has been a stable country**" for the past ten years under its current administration of President Pierre Nkurunziza, and the country "**has a tremendous amount to be proud of that [it] has accomplished**" during that decade. We are pleased that Burundi's accomplishments have been acknowledged by the U.S. government and look forward to hearing more words of encouragement like these.

For the past several weeks, Burundi has been on the front page of newspapers in Europe and North America. Some alarming analysis has appeared in the press that predicted an imminent humanitarian disaster – even civil war and genocide – that has not, in fact, occurred. There have been protests and tumult, to be sure, and some unfortunate deaths due to political violence that has, for the most part, been kept under control by the well-disciplined Burundian police force. The kinds of solutions proposed by those not near the situation seems to suggest that Burundi cannot learn from its own history.

To avoid simplistic analysis of the current situation in Burundi, it is necessary to remember that our country's Constitution, adopted in February 2005 by referendum, guarantees that all ethnic groups in the country are represented at all levels, in all the institutions of Burundi, according to the spirit of Arusha Agreement and the Global Cease Fire Agreement. Our Government has endeavored, for instance, to see that the military is ethnically balanced and diverse, so that no single ethnic group predominates, and matters of training and discipline are conducted in a colorblind fashion.

Let me underscore this: Our Government is strongly committed to respect the principle of broad representation in government and society, which is the cornerstone of national reconciliation, civil peace, and social stability in Burundi. The period of the ethnic exclusion established by military regimes in the past and which led to inter-ethnic cycle of violence is over. The Arusha Agreement and our 2005 Constitution were written to guarantee a peaceful, democratic 21st century that has discarded the violence and discord of the 20th century.

I am sure that your witnesses on Wednesday July 22rd, 2015 will discuss the controversy about whether President Nkurunziza is entitled to seek a second elected term as Burundi's Chief Executive. While we feel this matter was settled by the Constitutional Court on May 5th, 2015, it may be appropriate to provide you with some background information.

With regard to the term limit, Article 96 of the Constitution of Burundi states that: "**The President of the Republic is elected by universal direct suffrage for a mandate of five years renewable one time.**" The current crisis arose really from the interpretation of that article and it is normal that all Burundians have the right to discuss all the questions of national interest. Robust political debate, even about interpretation of a country's constitution, is a welcome and necessary component of a functioning democracy. There are, however, settled legal mechanisms authorized to decide how the Constitution should be interpreted and respected.

On May 5th, our Constitutional Court decided that President Nkurunziza is entitled to seek a second elected term. His first five years in office (from 2005 to 2010) were the result of appointment by Parliament, not election by universal suffrage.

President Nkurunziza has declared for the record – in fact, twice in speeches to the nation – that he will respect the decision of the Court and will not run in 2020. He will leave office at that time so that a successor, chosen by the people, can serve as President. If you have heard rumors that President Nkurunziza intends to stay in office for an unlimited time, that information is false. He is committed to the constitutional term limits and expects his successors in years to come to maintain the same commitment.

As you know, some political activists unfortunately decided to ignore the decision of the Court by organizing violent demonstrations in some neighborhoods of Bujumbura, Burundi's capital city. The failed military coup of May 13th, 2015, demonstrated that the main objective of those who planned the violent demonstrations were to interfere with the democratic, constitutionally-mandated electoral process and create conditions for taking power by unconstitutional means.

As soon as the military coup failed, agitators immediately reviewed their strategy and started to request for a transitional government instead of holding elections, according to the rule of law. For everyone who remembers the recent history of Burundi, the civil war of 1993 was the consequence of the assassination of the President-elect Melchior Ndadaye after only three months in office. The people of Burundi reacted violently against those who, through that assassination, refused to allow the people to be ruled by the government they voted for. It is also necessary to recall that the Transitional Government imposed immediately after that assassination did not prevent the military coup of 1996.

With all this as background, this is why, in the spirit of the Arusha Agreement, the Global Ceasefire and the Constitution of Burundi, and with the objective of avoiding chaos and civil unrest, the Government of Burundi organized local and parliamentary elections that were held on June 29th, 2015, the Presidential election held on July 21st, 2015, and a Senate election now scheduled for July 24th, 2015. Although some political parties boycotted these elections, their decision not to participate does not invalidate their legality, legitimacy, and fundamental democratic nature.

Our Government has made clear its intention to adhere to the rule of law and constitutional government, despite pressure by outside forces to delay elections unconstitutionally and threaten the democratic foundations of Burundi's government.

We have repeatedly said that outside observers from human rights organizations, the international news media, international institutions (such as the United Nations and the African Union), and our friends and allies abroad are free to come to Burundi to watch how our people vote, how the government and political parties respond to popular sovereignty, and how our institutions respect the rights of the people to govern themselves.

The Government of Burundi invites all our partners to respect the choice of the Burundian people and to clearly oppose and condemn any actions that could destabilize our country, our government, and our institutions.

With respect, Mr. Chairman, I request that this letter be included in the record of your subcommittee hearing scheduled for July 22nd, 2015.

Yours sincerely,

Ernest NDABASHINZE

AMBASSADOR

CC:

-Senator Jim Inhofe
- Senator Mike Rounds
- Rep. Vern Buchanan
- Rep. Joe Barton
- Rep. Ann Kirkpatrick
- Rep. Tim Walberg
- Rep. Bennie G. Thompson
- Rep. George K. Butterfield

Washington, D.C.

2233 Wisconsin avenue, NW., suite 408, Washington, DC, 20007- Tel. (202)342-2574, Fax:(202)342-2578,
E-mail: burundiembusadc@gmail.com, Website : burundiembassydc-usa.org

MATERIAL SUBMITTED FOR THE RECORD BY THE HONORABLE CHRISTOPHER H. SMITH, A REPRESENTATIVE IN CONGRESS FROM THE STATE OF NEW JERSEY, AND CHAIRMAN, SUBCOMMITTEE ON AFRICA, GLOBAL HEALTH, GLOBAL HUMAN RIGHTS, AND INTERNATIONAL ORGANIZATIONS

Department of Political Science
Mary Baldwin College
PO Box 1500
Staunton, Virginia 24402

Written Statement of

Cara E. Jones, PhD

Before the U.S. House of Representatives
Subcommittee on Africa, Global Health, Global Human Rights, and International
Organizations

July 22, 2015

Thank you to the House Subcommittee on Africa, Global Health, Global Human Rights, and International Organizations for convening this very timely and important hearing on "The Unfolding Crisis in Burundi," and for allowing me to introduce this statement into the record. I hold a doctorate in Political Science with a certificate in African Studies from the University of Florida (awarded May 2013), and am assistant professor of Political Science at Mary Baldwin College in Staunton, Virginia. I was a Fulbright-Hays Doctoral Dissertation Research Abroad fellow in Burundi in 2010-2011, and have worked on Burundian and Great Lakes politics since 2006. My publications and ongoing research focuses on the transitions that armed groups make to political power in the region and especially the CNDD-FDD (The National Council for the Defense of Democracy- Forces for the Defense of Democracy), the current ruling party of Burundi.

Summary

Burundi has been variously described as "on the brink"[1] and "in crisis," with warnings of "major instability"[2] in the upcoming weeks. From the announcement of incumbent President Pierre (Peter) Nkurunziza's candidacy for a third Presidential term on April 25, 2015, a series of violent and chaotic events rocked the country, culminating in more than 180,000 refugees[3], approximately 100 mostly opposition protestors and civilians dead, hundreds injured and imprisoned, and what looks to be the beginning of a regional crisis. This statement provides evidence and focuses on potential actions relating to the regional effects of the ongoing crisis. In particular, five issues are of note:

1) The expanding refugee problem for both Burundi and its neighbors
2) The potential for armed insurrection arising in Burundi and spilling over to neighbors, with potential interactions with additional armed groups operating in the region
3) Regional and East African Community (EAC) politics that underpin current mediations
4) The impact of Burundi's political crisis upon African Union (AU) politics and especially in regards to continuing African Union peacekeeping operations in which Burundi participates.

---

[1] Nkundwa, Jean Claude and Jonathan Rosen. 2015. "Burundi on the Brink" *The New York Times*. Available online
[2] Richardson, Paul. 2015. "UN Warns Burundi's vote likely to cause 'Major Instability'". *Bloomberg Business*. Available online < http://www.bloomberg.com/news/articles/2015-07-16/un-warns-burundi-vote-likely-to-result-in-major-instability->.
[3] According to UNHCR, there were 15,176 official refugees from before the crisis. Since 25 April, there are a reported 11,165 refugees in Uganda, 13,368 in the Democratic Republic of Congo, 65,181 in Rwanda, and 79,486 in Tanzania. Data updated 17 July 2015.

5) Potential constitutional changes across sub-Saharan Africa.

Introduction

A major ethnic civil war from 1993-2005 in Burundi displaced millions of Burundian citizens both internally and externally and killed over 300,000 with major long-term effects on the Central African state's economic, social, and political fabric. Post-conflict elections organized in 2005 were hailed as an important step in Burundi's recovery and a harbinger[4] of transition to peace, prosperity, and security for a population 'tired of war'[5]. Over the next 10 years, the CNDD-FDD government made great strides in post-conflict economic recovery, improvements on human development indicators, and building credibility among previously faltering institutions, especially the revenue authority and the FDN, the national army[6]. The 2010 elections, however, were marred by pre and post-election violence, with the CNDD-FDD and PALIPEHUTU-FNL accused of inter-group intimidations, killings, and beatings[7]. Observers however, found the first round of those elections to be generally in accordance with international electoral principles[8], although opposition parties found the results suspect and called for immediate boycott of the remaining elections, including the presidential. Thus, Nkurunziza ran all but unopposed in an election tarnished by killings and grenade attacks. The boycott of the 2010 election succeeded in shrinking political space in Burundi and paved the way for more CNDD-FDD programming funneled through the government, especially populist campaigns in rural areas, where the party and "Pita" (Nkurunziza) enjoy high popularity. Repression and violence continued even after the election, culminating in the attack on the Gatumba Bar Chez Les Amis[9] in September 2011. Development and trade faltered in the second CNDD-FDD regime, further contributing to deteriorating relationships between the government, civil society, and opposition political parties. A proposed constitutional amendment to change the number of terms a president may serve failed by one vote in March 2014, and further

---

[4] Peterson, Dave. 2006. "A Beacon for Central Africa." *Journal of Democracy* 17 (1):125-131.
[5] Jones, Cara. 2013. *Giving up the Gun: Rebel to Ruler Transitions in Africa's Great Lakes Region.* PhD Dissertation. University of Florida, chapter 2.
[6] Samii, Cyrus. 2013. "Perils of Promise of Ethnic Re-Integration: Evidence from a Hard Case". *American Political Science Review* 107 (3): 558-573.
[7] Ghoshal, Neela. 2010. "We will tie you up and shoot you: lack of accountability for political violence in Burundi" *Human Rights Watch* New York.
[8] Palmans, Eva. 2010. "Burundi's 2010 Elections: Democracy and Peace at Risk?" *European Centre for Electoral Support*
[9] "Burundi: Investigate Deadly Bar Shooting". 2011. *Human Rights Watch.* Available online < https://www.hrw.org/news/2011/09/20/burundi-investigate-deadly-bar-shooting>.

crackdown on political activities continued, including a ban on group exercise and assembly. Numerous protests broke out in 2015 before the April Anti-Third term manifestations, especially in Bujumbura, over issues like gas shortages, cell phone taxes, market and land ownership, and other economic frustrations. Several weeks into the anti-third term protests on May 13, 2015, while Nkurunziza was away at an EAC emergency heads of state meeting, a coup attempt was carried out by a group of former CNDD-FDD soldiers now serving in the national army. The coup failed to secure government infrastructures and was repelled by pro-Nkurunziza national police and armed forces within 48 hours. This led to more repression, crackdown on media freedoms, and killings of not only suspected putschists, but also those opposition and civil society figures now deemed 'insurgents' or putschist collaborators[10]. Many international organizations in Burundi have pulled programming, funding, and assistance, including the U.S. government. Protests and killings continue, and crisis has spilled over to the countryside. At the time of writing[11], Burundi is currently at an uneasy peace awaiting disputed presidential elections boycotted by opposition parties and deemed 'impossible' by nearly all international observers, and nearly 2% of the Burundian population are now refugees.

Refugee Issues

Because of Burundi's long history of violence (massacres in 1965, genocide against the Hutu population in 1972, more massacres in 1988 and 1991 followed by the civil war), refugee outflows from the country have remained a priority for Burundi's neighbors. Historically, Tanzania and Rwanda have absorbed the greatest number, leading to sometimes devastating consequences[12]. According to the UNHCR, most Burundians officially counted in the refugee statistics came after the breakout of the current protests (92.77%). There are perhaps thousands not included in statistics that are unofficial refugees, living abroad in Kigali, Kampala, and Brussels, among other places[13]. Despite extraordinary control measures by the government of Burundi, refugee outflows continue at rates of 1000-3000 per day, with surges before the parliamentary elections held on 29 June 2015 and expected the weekend before the Presidential

---

[10] Almost entirely inaccurate: the coup-plotters and civil society organizers had very little conversation before the coup was carried out and certainly were not mutually supportive (Personal Interview, 27 June 2015).
[11] July 18, 2015, four days before the scheduled Presidential elections.
[12] For example, the destabilization of the region in 1993 because of Burundi's war led to the Rwandan Genocide.
[13] Personal Interviews, 30 May 2015, 8 June 2015, and 17 July 2015.

election. Tanzania is perhaps the most well-equipped neighbor to handle refugees, as it hosts a large Burundian population since the Genocide of 1972 and currently serves both Congolese and Burundian refugee populations[14]. Rwanda has also acted quickly to provide resources and support to incoming refugees and has been quickly transiting those from border areas into more permanent camps.

Several issues must be addressed in the refugee crisis: material, financial, health and social support to hundreds of thousands of refugees, the possibility for more refugees (up to 300,000 as some experts suggest[15]), instability and factions along political lines within the camps themselves, and, historically, the linkages between refugees and rebellions in the region[16]. Additional aid has been promised by the United Nations and other donors[17], but the potential for the crisis to continue through the end of the year is high, and the United States government should prepare for additional support measures across all sectors. Support for returnees should also be a priority, as Burundi is largely dependent on subsistence agriculture. Additional food aid, support services, and health and education services should also be prepared. The dynamics of political conflict inside the camps must also be watched closely, as the likelihood of a civil war breaking out in Burundi also increases the likelihood of conflict and tension within the refugee camps themselves. Politics of the refugee-providing states may also impact these tensions. On the ground reporting and coordination, especially with Mr. Tom Perriello, the new Special Envoy for the Great Lakes, can mitigate potential information gaps and allow for more informed planning and response. Finally, more research is needed on the likelihood of refugees becoming rebels, a common phenomenon in the region. Investigating potential fault lines of conflict and finding evidence of armed groups will be key to avoiding future insurgencies.

New and Old Rebellions

As previously mentioned, the Burundi crisis has the potential to spawn new armed groups[18] operating against states in the region. Furthermore these armed groups may have

---

[14] "UNHCR: Burundi crisis propels refugee exodus" *Al-Jazeera* online at < http://www.aljazeera.com/news/2015/06/unhcr-burundi-crisis-propels-refugee-exodus-150626180155576.html>.
[15] ibid.
[16] Malkki, Liisa. *Purity and Exile: Violence, Memory, and National Cosmology among Hutu Refugees in Tanzania.* Chicago: U Chicago Press.
[17] "UN Steps up aid to Burundian Refugees" *Agence France Press* online at < http://news.yahoo.com/un-steps-aid-burundi-refugees-204909743.html>.
[18] Reports currently describe a brewing insurgency, as part of the 13 May attempted coup. Blair, Edmund. 2015. "Burundi's President faces an Armed Insurgency as Vote Looms" *Reuters*. Available online http://www.reuters.com/article/2015/07/13/us-burundi-politics-insurgency-analysis-idUSKCN0PN0SP20150713.

relationships with other armed non-state actors in the eastern part of the Democratic Republic of Congo (DRC), contributing to instability outside of Burundi's borders[19]. To date, the funding and details of the most recent rebel attack in Kayanza province on 13 July 2015 are scarce, with the government of Burundi reporting captured rebels originating from Nyungwe forest in Rwanda, but these reports lack independent verification and are disavowed by the Rwandan government[20]. With more promises of additional rebel attacks[21], the likelihood of continued violence is high. The United States government should focus intelligence gathering resources on monitoring these developments closely, taking care to investigate claims of inter-rebel relationships.

Regional Politics

Both the East African Community (EAC) and the African Union (AU) have great interests in supporting peaceful elections in Burundi. In recent weeks, as the EAC has continued to be the primary negotiating force, Uganda's President Yoweri Museveni has taken the lead, first in fostering and facilitating the regional meetings and then in facilitating mediation between opposition and the CNDD-FDD. Tanzania is thought to support the additional term for Nkurunziza, as a stability inducing measure that would affect neighbors politically, economically, and socially. Uganda is also thought to support Nkurunziza's candidacy[22]. There seems to be very few reasons for any regional players to support rebellion in Burundi or any other destabilizing actions, including the failed 13 May coup, although Rwanda especially has condemned violence by the regime and warned against violence against civilians[23]. There is little interest in military intervention by regional actors, and unilateral action seems highly unlikely given current conditions. Furthermore, all countries in the region have interests in continuing the EAC integration project, which has struggled to fully integrate Burundi across

---

[19] Nimubona, Desire. "Burundi Army kills 31 Suspected Rebels in Northern Forest" *Bloomberg News*. Available online < http://www.bloomberg.com/news/articles/2015-07-13/burundi-military-kills-31-suspected-rebels-in-northern-forest> .

[20] "Rwanda denies Claim of Providing Refuge to Armed Burundi Rebels" *The East African*. Available online http://mobile.theeastafrican.co.ke/News/Rwanda-denies-claims-of-refuge-to-armed-Burundi-rebels-/-/433842/2793388/-/format/xhtml/-/k3k6p1/-/index.html.

[21] "Rebels held, Arms Seized in Burundi" *Agence France Press*. Available online < http://news.yahoo.com/burundi-arrests-rebels-seizes-arms-ahead-presidential-poll-092236832.html>.

[22] Iaccino, Ludovica. 2015. "Burundi Coup: What do neighbouring countries think of Nkurunziza's third term bid?" *International Business Times UK*. Available online < http://www.ibtimes.co.uk/burundi-violence-what-do-neighbouring-countries-think-nkurunzizas-third-term-bid-1500980> .

[23] Iaccino and Opening Remarks by H.E. President Paul Kagame, International Conference for the Protection of Civilians in Peacekeeping Operations, May 29, 2015.

several dimensions. The United States government should be willing to provide technical assistance and support for human rights and electoral monitoring for the EAC and work with partner governments to ensure stability of the regional body. Furthermore, increased attention must be paid to post-election integration activities in the EAC to further ensure that the Burundian population does not suffer economic hardships. In the African Union (AU), several expressions of concern have been issued over the past two months: condemnation of the coup[24], doubts over the freedom and fairness of the parliamentary elections[25] and the deployment of military and human rights observers[26]. Support to the major intergovernmental organization on the African continent is crucial at this time, especially given the important relationship between Burundi and the African Union in various peacekeeping missions across the continent.

Other Third Terms in the Region and in sub-Saharan Africa

Nkurunziza's potential third term will be a test of the constitutionality and outcome of several proposed third term elections upcoming, not only in the Great Lakes but across Africa. In 2016, Joseph Kabila presumably will seek a third term in the DRC, and the Rwandan parliament recently approved measures allowing for Paul Kagame to seek a third term in 2017. Congo-Brazzaville's Denis Nguesso received approval to run for another term last week[27]. With the explosion of potentially termless presidents, the United States government must thoughtfully engage on questions of respect of original term limits, constitutional protectoral bodies, constitutional amendments and referendums, and political changeover, not only in the case of Burundi, but also in Burundi's test for other presumed third term presidents. The United States government must also engage with civil societies and oppositions in these cases to ensure free, fair, and peaceful elections and that ideas of democratic competition find solid footing.

Conclusion

---

[24] *The Peace and Security Council of the African Union (AU) decision on the situation in Burundi.* 14 May 2015. Available online < http://au.int/en/content/peace-and-security-council-african-union-au-decision-situation-burundi>.
[25] Manirabarusha, Clement. 2015. "African Union says elections in Burundi not free or fair, Speaker Flees" Available online < http://www.reuters.com/article/2015/06/28/us-burundi-politics-africanunion-idUSKCN0P80YD20150628>.
[26] *The African Union reaffirms the imperative for dialogue and consensus in order to peacefully resolve the current crisis in Burundi* 08 July 2015. Available online < http://cpauc.au.int/en/content/african-union-reaffirms-imperative-dialogue-and-consensus-order-peacefully-resolve-current-crisis-burundi> .
[27] "Burundi, Rwanda, and now Congo: another African President set to change term-limit rules" *Mail and Guardian Africa.* Available online < http://m.mgafrica.com/article/2015-07-18-burundi-rwanda-and-now-congo-another-african-president-set-to-get-a-third-term-and-more#.VaxuaUtZ8uk> .

While the likelihood of civil conflict and mass violence re-emerging in Burundi may be low, it is certainly not negligible[28]. It seems very likely that presidential elections will be carried out on 22 July 2015 in Burundi and that President Pierre Nkurunziza will win re-election. The United States government must take appropriate steps to address potential violence during the electoral period, refugee outflows from Burundi during the crisis, post-conflict returnees, and the regional and continental effects. Above all, the United States government and her people must reaffirm our commitment to the goal of safe, peaceful, and prosperous lives for the Burundian people who remain the most affected by the crisis.

---

[28] "Early Warning Project: Protests in Burundi and the Risk of Mass Killing". 02 May 2015. Available online www.earlywarningproject.com/2015/05/02/protests-in-burundi-and-the-risk-of-mass-killing>.

www.ingramcontent.com/pod-product-compliance
Lightning Source LLC
Chambersburg PA
CBHW081239280526
45787CB00006B/2728